Hamlyn all-colour paperbacks

Wargames

David Nash

D1613167

Hamlyn
London · New York · Sydney · Toronto

FOREWORD

This book seeks to provide the reader with an outline of wargaming. A single volume cannot do justice to such an extensive subject, but none the less I have referred to all its varied aspects, discussed the many forms that it has taken over the years, and placed it in its historical context.

The bulk of the book is concerned with what I have chosen to call the amateur's game, that which is now widely practised as a hobby. The intention is that by relating the factual data to be found in the second part of this book to game logic, which is discussed at length in the preceding sections, the reader can create his own games upon completely logical lines.

Although only three periods have been analyzed, the principles of wargaming are valid for any age. It cannot be overstressed that the foundation of a good wargame is a detailed knowledge of the chosen historical period. With this in mind, the reader's attention is drawn to the bibliography on pages 124–5. The titles mentioned therein will provide much of the additional historical information that could not be incorporated into this book through lack of space.

D.N.

Published by The Hamlyn Publishing Group Limited
London · New York · Sydney · Toronto
Astronaut House, Feltham, Middlesex, England

Copyright © The Hamlyn Publishing Group Limited 1974
ISBN 0 600 39269 4

Phototypeset in England by Filmtype Services Limited, Scarborough
Colour separations in England by Colour Workshop, Hertford
Printed in Spain by Mateu Cromo, Madrid

CONTENTS

THE HISTORY OF WARGAMING

From early times to 1807

Although, to many, wargaming would seem to be an activity of the twentieth century, its origins are to be found in antiquity. The exact point at which man first tried to simulate warfare as a game will always be open to conjecture, but it was certainly some thousands of years before Christ.

The first games all seem to have been dominated by a strategic objective, such as outflanking an opponent, as in the ancient Chinese game of wei-hai, or the capture of the centre of power, as personified by the King in a game of chess. Another ancient form of wargame was chaturanga. This Hindu game, although related to chess, required four players; its pieces represented specific warriors, on horse, elephant, foot, and in chariots. None of these games has a close connection with the type of wargaming described in the body of this book, but all won considerable acceptance in their time and wei-hai and chess are still widely practised today.

It was in Europe that the early forms of wargame gradually took on a more sophisticated appearance. During the seventeenth century several variations upon the basic game of chess were introduced. In 1644 Christopher Weikhmann developed his so-called 'King's Chess', with sixty pieces representing the military hierarchy from king to private soldier. This game had fourteen fixed moves.

During the eighteenth century a number of games were introduced into France which departed from the idea of pieces and which used series of cards designed to impart basic military knowledge to the players. Also, at about this time, silver model soldiers were being used at the French Court to instruct the future king, Louis XIV, in the art of war.

A prominent date in the evolution of wargaming is 1780, for in that year Helwig, Master of Pages to the Duke of Brunswick, produced a game which broke through the narrow limits to which wargaming had previously been confined. He seems to have been the first man to realize that markers on a miniature battlefield need not necessarily represent individual soldiers. His game was indeed impressive. It had pieces representing most of the components of full-scale armies and many of the elements of the modern amateur's game were included, such as the different movement values of infantry, cavalry, and the supporting arms. However, its concept was still geared to a grid system, although considerably larger than that previously used, numbering no less than 1,666 squares, and with provision for five kinds of terrain.

It seems likely that Helwig's game was developed and some twenty years later Viturinus presented a limited and bewildered public with what was surely the ultimate in complexity: a game played on 3,600 squares and with some 2,500 pieces. This 'Neues Kriegsspiel', as it was known, was governed by sixty pages of rules which seem to have been incomprehensible to its players!

Wargaming in Prussia

A significant side-effect of the Napoleonic Wars, and one which went almost unnoticed at the time, was the birth of the Prussian military machine. Although Prussia had a glorious military tradition, mainly won during the reign of Frederick the Great, it was the reformers under Scharnhorst and

Whilst still a boy, Louis XIV was taught the principles of warfare with a set of silver soldiers.

Gneisenau who laid the foundation for later German military greatness. Amongst other innovations was a staff system headed by dedicated men who were ready to seize upon any idea to improve the training and efficiency of their army and officers.

In 1811 Herr von Reisswitz of Berlin received Prussian royal patronage for his newly-invented wargame. What von Reisswitz had done was simply evolve a wargame governed by realistic rules, in which units were represented by blocks operated on a relief model sculpted to a scale of twenty-six inches to a mile, thus breaking away from the idea of a squared board.

The immediate cause of the Prussian King's interest was the enthusiasm of his two sons, Frederick and William. In the following year, however, when Reisswitz presented an improved version of his game, the King became instantly addicted. It was said that the King together with the Prince of Mecklenburg would play into the small hours of the morning to complete a game.

Frederick William III and the Prince of Mecklenburg playing the game devised by the older Reisswitz. In Prussia, wargaming developed into a popular military pastime.

Von Reisswitz's son, an artillery officer, revised the game and modified the rules by substituting a map scaled at eight inches to the mile for the relief model. He also refined the unit blocks and introduced a die to represent the element of chance which is always present in warfare. In 1824 he was requested to demonstrate his system before Prince William, who was then the commander of a guards' division. This led to interest by the General Staff and, although the idea was initially scorned by von Müffling, the Chief of Staff, at the end of the game the old warrior declared, 'It's not a game at all; it's training for war.' Within days, the *Militär Wochenblatt* stated Müffling's approval and a royal order was given to all units that they were to procure Reisswitz's wargame, the expense being defrayed by the Military Finance Department.

Thus was the wargame introduced into the Prussian service. It was enthusiastically accepted by the officer corps and from then on numerous wargame clubs, the *Kriegsspiel Verein*, mushroomed in the garrison towns of Germany.

Wargaming, by its very nature, cannot stand still, and under the professional eyes of the German officer corps it progressed until by about 1870 it had split into two distinct types of game. The so-called 'Rigid *Kriegsspiel*' was thought to be useful only in the training of junior officers. Fixed rules, even with the use of dice, it was reasoned, were too rigid for the complicated problems of high command, and so what became known as 'Free *Kriegsspiel*' was used by senior officers. The essential difference was that instead of rules determining the outcome of each engagement, the result was adjudicated by highly qualified umpires. The use of umpires had been well established in the younger Reisswitz's time, but during the post-1870 period they absolutely dominated Free *Kriegsspiel*, adjudicating on all matters that were not related to mathematically proven fact.

The spread of Prussian wargaming
From Prussia the wargame rapidly spread through Germany and beyond. A fervent wargamer, and later a field marshal, Helmuth Carl Bernhard von Moltke, took *Kriegsspiel* to Turkey when he was attached to the Sultan's Army in the 1830s. The period from the Franco-Prussian War to the outbreak of the

Moltke took wargaming from Prussia to Turkey in the 1830s.

First World War saw wargaming accepted by all European and North American powers. The methods of victorious armies are often studied and this possibly helped the spread of *Kriegsspiel* to other armies. Be that as it may, by 1914 wargames were generally accepted as an aid to officer training.

Under the auspices of the British War Office, the game rules were translated into English, and, although in Britain *Kriegsspiel* never enjoyed the popularity that it had in Germany, it none the less had many devotees, mainly in the volunteer movement. Eminent amongst British wargamers was Spenser Wilkinson, who translated and wrote extensively on the subject, seeing it as a way to rectify what he considered to be the lamentable state of training amongst volunteer officers.

One of the most significant early names in American wargaming was that of Major W. R. Livermore, whose wargame rules, first published in 1879, provided for a detailed game

which was completely realistic. Modern players have accused Livermore of making his game too complicated, but it was devised with the intention of being simple, so that it could easily be played in the small American garrison towns, many of which were no more than frontier settlements.

The few names mentioned above were amongst the leading exponents of military wargaming during the so-called 'hundred years of peace', but it should not be imagined that the experts were a small band of men. There were wargame theorists by the thousand. Many put their ideas on paper and, although pamphlets and books dating from the period are not easily available today, they still exist in national archives. Most of the German *Kriegsspiel Verein* produced sets of rules sufficiently different from the accepted military standard to be regarded as separate. Societies existed in all the countries to which wargaming had spread, and the period immediately prior to the First World War would undoubtedly have been known as the golden age of wargaming, but for the phenomenal upsurge of interest in the late 1960s.

Wargaming's effect on warfare

Although wargaming was seen as an aid to officer training, there came a time when it was regarded as being so realistic that a new role was found for it. Planning operations with the help of wargaming seems to have been a natural offshoot of the German Free *Kriegsspiel*. It was reasoned that if all the latest data relating to mobilization plans, troop dispositions, and so on were taken into account, then a wargame based upon these facts could predict with considerable accuracy the likely course of any war. Thus the Germans argued, and the Schlieffen Plan was a direct result of military planning and discussion coupled with predictions of enemy reactions as based on a protracted series of wargames. Alfred von Schlieffen was the Chief of the German General Staff from 1892 to 1906 and his plan proposed the advance of German forces through Belgium in the event of war with France. Although numerous games were played to test the efficiency of such matters as the railway's contribution to mobilization, there

The German offensive of 1918 was the result of planning based on a series of wargames.

were grave doubts about the feasibility of his plans. None the less, they formed the basis of German operations in August 1914.

Another game of great importance was the British game of 1905. It set out to consider the implications of a German invasion through Belgium and its results led to the conclusion that the Belgium Army was not strong enough to garrison its many fortresses and also to operate in the field. It predicted the successful German advance through Belgium but drew attention to the fact that there were weaknesses in any German plan to invade France through Flanders because of the inadequacies of the Belgium railway system. British involvement was built into the game and it was concluded that Britain's power lay in a naval blockade of Germany and not in providing a large field army for operations on the continent. The 1905 wargame provided the basis for British military planning up to 1914 and led to the Anglo-French military discussions in the period prior to the outbreak of the First World War.

Although wargames certainly held lessons when based upon undoubted fact, there came a point beyond which the results were highly suspect. As can be seen from the above, the

strategic conclusions drawn from wargaming were far from satisfactory. Military wargames did not take account of international diplomacy, nor could they foresee the improbable. The German armies that marched into Belgium in 1914 certainly did not realize that they would still be fighting four years later because, it could be argued, of a misplaced belief in the visionary properties of the wargame. In brief, it would seem that only wargames with a tactical or a limited strategic objective are of military use.

However, the Germans still placed a great deal of faith in wargaming. Operation Michael, the great offensive of 1918, was proven by a wargame to stand only a very slender chance of decisive success, but it was a chance worth taking by a country which was facing undoubted defeat without such a gamble.

Between the wars, German officers continued to play wargames and serious attention was given to the political aspects of strategy, the Foreign Ministry even becoming involved in an official capacity. One of the more famous names connected with wargaming at this time was that of Erich von Manstein, later to rise to the rank of field marshal.

Under Hitler, wargames were made obligatory for regimental officers; they were to be played on one night of each week during the winter. Wargaming also progressed at a higher level. Wargame study-groups were given specific problems by the General Staff and one of the games predicted that the invasion of Czechoslovakia would probably lead to a catastrophe for Europe and Germany. So convinced of the accuracy of these findings was Ludwig Beck, the Chief of Staff, that he resigned his post.

During the Second World War, the experience of the *Wehrmacht* in Poland in 1939 was utilized to create wargames based on the plan to invade France through the Ardennes. Operation Sealion, the proposed invasion of Great Britain, and Barbarossa, the invasion of Russia, were amongst other projects rehearsed on the wargame table. It is said that in 1944 while the attack through the Ardennes was in progress a game was, by chance, running in parallel; the situation reports were transferred to the wargame table and the table moves were used as actual orders to the front-line troops.

Japanese torpedo aircraft. The torpedoes used at Pearl Harbor were modified to run in shallow water after a wargame had proven this particular requirement.

An interesting example of wargame miscalculation is provided by the Japanese in the Pacific. Their early successes were all planned with the use of politico-military wargaming, as was the projected assault upon Midway Island. The play of the Midway game seems to have been biased in the Japanese favour by the umpires and the result led to a rather optimistic view of the possibilities. However, during the actual operation something unpredicted happened – the Americans intercepted Japanese radio messages and were able to concentrate their forces so that the assault went awry. What was to have been another victory in a run of success turned out to be the first crushing defeat suffered by the Japanese, and the large naval losses inflicted on them during this action cost them the war.

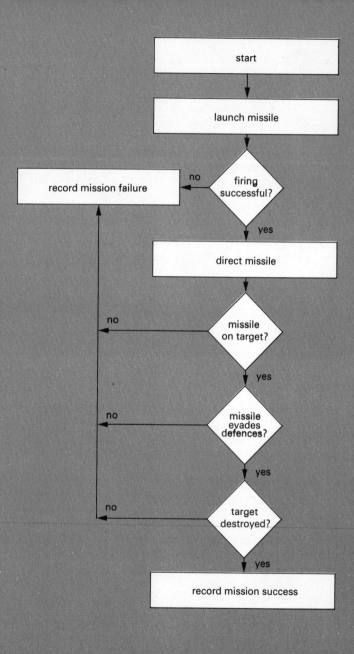

Modern wargaming

During the Second World War, mathematicians began to study weapon performance. By analyzing numerous identical situations they were able to provide a statistical basis for weapon usage and tactics. An early example of this logic had occurred in 1915 when the high incidence of head wounds resulted in the introduction of steel helmets, but it was not until the Second World War that these principles were fully understood and exploited. It then became possible to apply mathematics to any given situation and to provide a statistical answer to questions such as 'how efficient are bomb sights?' or 'how effective are torpedoes?'

The principles developed by what was known as 'operational research' provided a firm foundation for the post-war advance of wargaming. This, and the advent of the computer, revolutionized the official wargame. Today, wargaming is as much used as it ever was, perhaps more so. Whole American institutions have been turned over to its study, but the cost is now measured in millions of dollars, and there is no reason to believe that the situation in Russia is any different at all.

Vietnam is, to date, the most gamed war in history, but the results of games based upon that situation will be rated alongside those that influenced Schlieffen. All seem to have led to strategic blunders of the first magnitude. Thus it is probably fair to restate the wargaming position as it was a century ago. The wargame is valuable only when it is based upon proven fact. Introduce an unknown element and its results are subject to doubt.

In the final analysis, however, is this imperfect method worse than any other in determining military policy in a highly complex world? On balance, wargaming will, no doubt, continue at its present level since no other method exists to judge the factors which make up the contemporary international power structure.

A flow chart from a computer wargame. In constructing a detailed representation of a computer game, the activity and interrelation of many items have to be considered. On the basis of this chart, a program will be set up to examine the performance of long-range missiles fitted with inertial guidance systems.

The amateur's wargame

Apart from the early history of the wargame, we have so far been concerned with what might be termed 'professional' wargaming, and this has been included to give the reader an insight into the origins of table-top warfare. The period 1870 to 1914 is of particular relevance since at that time the professional game was easily within the reach of all interested persons. The cost was minute when compared to modern official wargaming, and essentially the amateur's game springs from that time.

Early enthusiasts of note were R. L. Stevenson and H. G. Wells. Wells wrote a book entitled *Little Wars* and its publication was a major milestone in amateur wargaming. The book, which was illustrated with line drawings of William Britain's toy soldiers, described essentially a child's game. Wells in fact dedicated it to 'boys of all ages . . .'. In the first half of the twentieth century, many individuals either modified Wells's game or invented their own, but it was really only in the mid-1950s that amateur wargaming at large began to evolve from a hobby which most people considered infantile into its present-day status as a sophisticated pastime.

The early amateur games were mostly governed by simple rules and dice. There was little relationship between the game and reality, except in the minds of the players. In fact, Wells's legacy hindered serious wargaming because of its essentially child-like approach to the subject. Advanced players did, of course, exist at that time, but they were usually in complete isolation.

One of the first unifying forces in the hobby was an American magazine entitled *The War Game Digest*. Its first issue was published in 1957 and it soon attracted numerous readers throughout the English-speaking world. This journal provided a platform for discussion and a medium through which wargamers could contact each other. In fact, it is true to say that the people who contributed so much to the wargaming upsurge in the 1960s were brought together mostly through the columns of this magazine.

By the mid-1960s, sufficient contact had been established between individual wargamers, and enough converts had been made for several wargame clubs to be formed and for an increasing quantity of literature to be produced on the subject. Conventions and national championships attracted a great deal of publicity and did much to alter the public's attitude to wargaming.

Amateur wargames were traditionally fought with a 54mm scale figure, as produced by William Britain. This scale is not convenient for wargaming (see page 27) and the hobby owes much to the different manufacturers who successively lowered the scale until today 20mm is the almost universal figure-scale used in wargames. The advent of plastic soldiers, much mourned by many figure collectors, made masses of cheap figures available to wargamers and the rise of amateur wargaming may, in some ways, be due to their production.

Thus, since the mid-1960s, the organizational structure laid down by the veteran wargamers, the availability of cheap plastic 20mm figures, and the ever-increasing literature on the subject, have produced a situation in which few cities do not have active wargame clubs; others exist in schools and universities, and the groups of wargamers who meet on an informal basis are too numerous to be counted.

H. G. Wells was a keen wargamer and the author of the classic work *Little Wars*.

THE BASIC WARGAME

Wargames are devised to suit the circumstances of the player or players. Game construction is inescapably geared to such factors as the number of players, the size of the table, and the quantity of model soldiers and equipment available. Perhaps the most crucial factor of all is the attitude of the individual player because this ultimately overrides all other considerations. He may see his wargame as an affair of model soldiers, or, perhaps, of markers. The table-top encounter may be regarded as complete in itself, or it may fit into a larger scheme. Furthermore, it is the player's attitude which determines whether the game will be truly realistic or whether it will be played casually, merely for its 'entertainment' value.

Whatever the player's inclination, table-top warfare conveniently divides into three elements: terrain, figures, and rules. As will be seen, these three elements have a definite interrelationship in a well-constructed game, being linked together by common ground and time scales.

Most wargamers are adept at making their own layouts.

Terrain

The terrain can be defined as the area upon which a wargame is played. It can take the form of a map, grid, or model layout. The latter is, however, the most popular, and it is generally mounted upon a table top.

Table size is sensibly governed by the distance that an arm can be extended so as to reach figures in its centre, and a table width of some six feet results. Length is not covered by any such considerations, but if the table is very long the game tends to become unbalanced. Thus, in normal circumstances, one is more or less forced to adopt a table which is about six feet by nine feet, a size which fits conveniently into most rooms.

The ground scale of the terrain is of supreme importance since it determines the accurate rendering of weapon ranges and, when coupled with the time scale, of troop movements. In determining a ground scale, several factors must be borne in mind – figure scale is the most significant, and this is explained on page 28; suffice it to say for the moment that there must be a link between the area occupied by a formation and the chosen ground scale. The obvious scale is one in which a model soldier represents its own size, but this is usually considered to be impracticable since it calls for units of up to a thousand figures and prohibitive weapon ranges reaching from one side of a table to the other.

Since two armies are to be marshalled on the table top, and room is obviously required for manoeuvre, the scale is, of necessity, relatively small. Popular ground scales amongst players are 1 inch to 25, 33, or 50 yards, a convenient alternative to the first being 1 millimetre to 1 yard. All these scales produce units with a manageable number of figures and ample space on a normal table to manoeuvre. However, other scales should not be disregarded. On a game employing markers, the scale can be very much smaller and there are times when the actual figure scale, noted earlier, may be preferred.

Determining a ground scale does not necessarily dictate the size of terrain features since it is only the ground area which relates to this scale. For aesthetic reasons a vertical scale in proportion to the type of figures employed is usually adopted when adding buildings and other features to the game area.

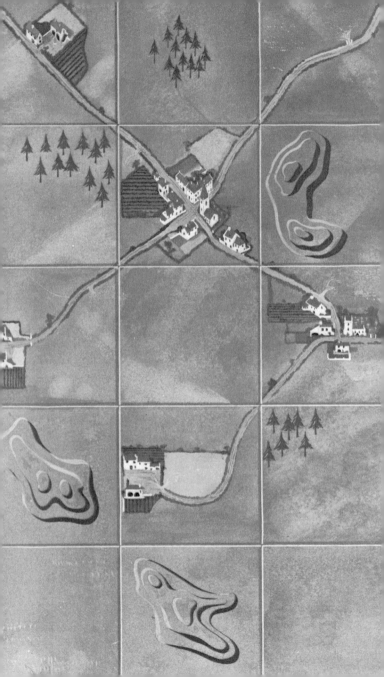

Wargames based upon model figures are usually played on a terrain which includes miniature houses, walls, hedges, trees, and so on. So exact are some of these layouts that they are marvellous modelling feats in their own right.

The 'ground' can be sculpted from blocks of expanded polystyrene to represent the desired natural features and then painted accordingly. One of the skills in creating a terrain like this is to design it so as to make the pieces interchangeable, thus providing an infinite number of layout combinations from fifteen or eighteen basic blocks. This type of layout is seen as ideal by many wargamers, but it has one serious defect: it is very difficult to transport owing to its bulk and can really only be used in a permanent wargame room.

This is why a single flat table-top is the most popular ground for a wargame. Natural features can be added to a flat surface, achieving the same result as in a sculpted model layout, but without the same realism. Hills can be simulated by a series of cutouts, in wood or polystyrene, each one representing a contour. Complete hills can be made, but the former method is often favoured since the area between each contour is flat, thus enabling model figures to stand upright. Rivers and roads are often represented simply by laying coloured strips of cloth on the table in the required fashion. When setting up a layout of this nature, it is wise to cover the table top in some way. Green fabric makes a good base and can be said to represent grass. The natural features are placed on top of this. If a wargamer wishes to represent more than just ground, water, and roads, additional coloured cloth can be introduced. Ploughed fields, for instance, are a useful auxiliary feature since they restrict movement, particularly of wheeled transport, and they can be realistically simulated by pieces of brown corduroy. Marshy ground can likewise be represented by a distinctive area.

As previously mentioned, artificial and natural terrain features are generally in scale with the figures employed on the table, but the base area must fit into the overall ground scale. Thus, a village is portrayed by one or two houses and a

A terrain made from interlocking blocks. These can be positioned in various ways, thus providing a number of different layouts.

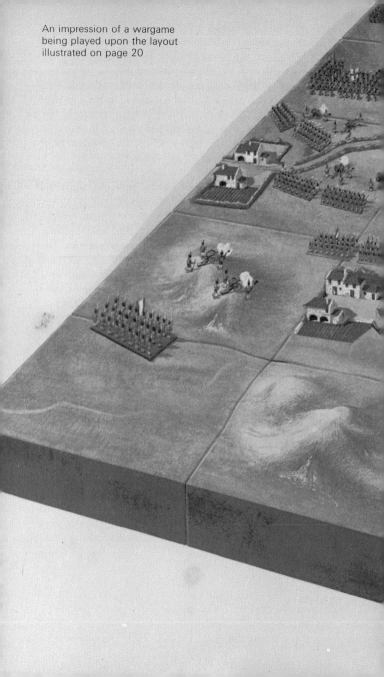

An impression of a wargame
being played upon the layout
illustrated on page 20

wood by a small clump of trees. By adopting this logic, the layout is made pleasing to the eye without upsetting the ground scale.

Houses can easily be made from card, or there are many miniature buildings available in kit form. Trees can be made from wood and lichen, or plastic ones can be purchased. Hedges, fences, walls, haystacks, etc. can all be constructed at a minimal cost with a little imagination. Many wargamers devote a great deal of time to their miniature soldiers, but their efforts are very often completely neutralized by second-rate layouts. It is worth paying attention to the construction of model scenery since an effective terrain definitely enhances a wargame table.

A few wargamers opt for sand tables instead of the type of layout just described. The sand table has the advantage that it can be sculpted to any shape, providing the sand is damp; the auxiliary features can then be placed on the finished surface. Its great disadvantage is, however, its enormous weight for this makes it completely immovable – indeed often the floor has to be reinforced if the table is large.

Some thought should be given to the use of features before they are laid down. There is a natural tendency to overcrowd a wargame table with hills and villages, a combination which always causes a game to degenerate into a struggle for these key points. The reason for this is fairly simple: the defenders of such positions always hold an advantage over the attackers. However, to win, such locations must be stormed so it is wise to leave a reasonable amount of open space for manoeuvre.

Another common mistake is for each side to hold such geographically strong front-lines that whoever attacks is bound to be defeated. There is much to be said for the belief that geography determines the relative weight of opposing forces. In fact whole games can be governed by this principle. A strong army, for instance, can be given the objective of attacking a weaker one which holds the advantages of terrain, or is even perhaps entrenched.

Modelling the layout of an actual battle and scaling the forces to those that were involved is a useful exercise from which one learns a great deal.

For those who prefer a less complicated terrain, there are

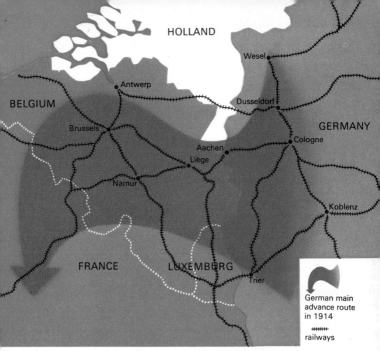

It was on maps of this area that the British Staff Game of 1905 was fought, and it predicted that a German advance through Belgium would fail because of its dependence upon a single railway line from Aachen to Liège.

maps, grids, and boards upon which to play. Maps and map scales depend very much upon the scope of the game to be played. Units of soldiers have usually to be represented by markers in map games. This is because the map scale – and the resulting ground scale – require it. On the other hand it is possible to devise map games based on such a large scale that the markers become individual soldiers.

The mechanics of a map game are similar to those of a game played on a model layout. What is different, however, is that on a model the game is confined to the table area, whereas with maps there is no such limit. Complete campaigns, with all the complications of supply and manoeuvre, can easily be reproduced on a map. When an outflanking move is under-way, there is no question of it stopping at the edge of a map.

Additional map sheets provide the automatic answer. One is really forced to the conclusion, despite the pre-occupation of contemporary wargamers, that map games, as used by general staffs at the turn of the century, are more realistic, cheaper to produce, easier to store and transport, and more logical in their execution and outcome.

The use of a terrain composed of boards requires a completely different type of game structure. It must invariably be a stylized chess-type game since boards are always divided into geometrically equal sections. Groupings of these squares, octagons, or whatever, can be distinctively marked so as to

A diversity of miniatures is available to the wargamer.

provide geographic features, but board games can do little more than provide an enjoyable game based upon a broad interpretation of military history. Some are virtually games of chance, whereas others are very definitely games of skill, but the skill is in interpreting and practising the rules of the game itself.

Grid games are like board games in some respects but there is also a place for grids in realistic table-top warfare. The superimposition of a grid reference system over a conventional wargame table has its uses, particularly in a modern wargame where so much reliance is placed upon map references for artillery fire and air strikes. Grid systems also provide instant measurements so that rulers need not always be referred to when moving pieces. Perhaps grids are most valuable when dealing with the unknown. References to concealed troops can be noted down and submarine and aerial warfare is simplified by the use of a grid.

Finally, it is a good idea to discuss and note down the direction in which rivers flow and in which way the wind is blowing. Broken pontoon bridges for instance would drift downstream, and black-powder smoke would drift with the wind, providing a dense blanket through which no one could see.

Figures

The figures are the individual pieces which are used upon the terrain to represent the forces employed. They range from the simple pieces of card, or wooden blocks, used on maps to delicately painted miniatures of soldiers and equipment. Whatever type of figure is used, the ground area that it occupies must match the ground scale of the game in which it is used. This point cannot be overstressed.

With card markers and blocks, this is simply achieved by reckoning the dimensions of a given type of unit and then equating these with the game ground scale. For instance, a Napoleonic battalion in a column of divisions had an actual frontage of 50 yards and a depth of 15 yards. If the ground scale employed is 1 inch to 25 yards, then the piece which represents the battalion should be $2 \times \frac{3}{5}$ inches. The same battalion will cover various ground areas depending upon

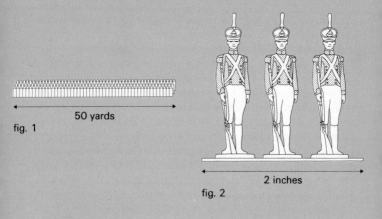

fig. 1

50 yards

fig. 2

2 inches

A company of 150 soldiers, drawn into three ranks, had a frontage
of approximately fifty yards, as shown in figure 1. Figure 2 shows
three model soldiers would occupy a 2-inch frontage. When related,
these two particular examples produce a ground scale of 1 inch to
25 yards and a figure scale of 1 to 50.

the type of formation into which it is drawn – line, column of
route, and so on – but with differently sized pieces all of these
formations can be accurately denoted.

Most wargamers, however, prefer to use 20mm or 30mm
miniature soldiers, and these are grouped into units governed
by a rigid figure scale, one model figure representing perhaps
twenty-five or fifty soldiers and their stands equalling the
area occupied by a company or battalion. It is not always
possible to gain an exact unit area/scale ratio, as can be done
with markers, because the base depth of these figures is
irreconcilable to the depth of most military formations unless
a ground scale in the order of 1 inch to 10 yards is employed.
This would require a figure scale of about one to ten, resulting
in infantry battalions of fifty to a hundred men, too large for
use on a standard-sized wargame table. Most wargamers opt
for units of between twelve and twenty-four figures.

In choosing a figure scale, it is also important to remember that there is considerable scope for elasticity since the total number of men in any military unit is never constant. Casualties and the difficulty of obtaining replacements often means that units are little stronger than fifty per cent of their establishment.

For ease of movement in a wargame, model figures can be fixed on to bases. These bases then represent the area occupied by the unit. To overcome the manoeuvring problems which would result if a whole battalion or regiment were stuck to a common base, it is wise to select either a platoon or company as the basic unit. The sub-units of a battalion or whatever can

For ease of movement it is convenient to mount figures in the manner shown. In this Napoleonic example, each block represents a company, and the six companies form a battalion.

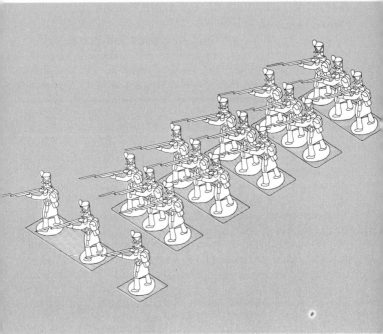

then be moved so as to cater for any type of manoeuvre – whether it be column, line, or square. However, by judicious use of single figures carried on the common base and not stuck to it, even skirmishing lines can be drawn up in the prescribed manner.

For modern warfare it is usually accepted that one piece represents just one piece, although it may well be part of a particular organizational structure. This is because there has been a change in the form of warfare. Up to about 1860, unit cohesion was of paramount importance, but thereafter improved weapon technology increasingly demanded a much looser type of warfare.

Equipment for model armies is available from a variety of sources. Today there are plastic kits to satisfy even the most demanding wargamer, but there is still a place for the older practice of constructing one's own equipment from card, paper, and sheet plastic.

Wargame rules

Wargame rules control the movements and encounters of figures upon a terrain and, as with the basic game concept, they invariably reflect the players' attitude. The one consistent factor is that they are in a constant state of flux since, no matter how carefully they are compiled, they are always being revised in the light of new factual data discovered by the players, or because certain rules may not, in practice, provide the desired effect, or because an entirely new game concept has been discovered. An elementary, but often overlooked, step before commencing a wargame is to check that the players all have the same set of rules, complete with the appropriate amendments.

A wargamer needs several items to interpret a set of rules properly. Since both movement and fire effect are always coupled to distance, it is wise to have a good-quality expanding steel-ruler. The usual length is 60 inches, but it can also be obtained with metric gradations. Dice play an important part in most wargames. Many wargamers use what have been termed 'average dice'. These are dice on which the one and the six are removed and replaced by an additional three and four. A one and a six represent such disastrously bad and incredibly good results on the battlefield that they happen seldom enough to be of little consequence. Removing them tends to produce average results and eliminate the wild fluctuations of luck that can occur on a wargame table. Protractors are also useful since they can measure the limits of artillery traverse. A gun can only be swung so far without actually being re-positioned and this obviously affects its firepower since the crew must stop working the piece to manhandle it on to a new target.

It is normal game procedure for the opposing forces to be set out on the table, whereupon the players start to move their pieces. The move (or period or bound, as it is sometimes known) can be either alternate or simultaneous. Alternate moves make for a slower game and allow time for the player whose army is static to prepare the next move in his mind. Simultaneous moves speed up a game and allow less time for thought. When both sides have moved, the fire effect is calculated and, if necessary, the results of engagements decided.

The reference to 'thought' stems from the inescapable fact that the players look down upon the battlefield with all-seeing eyes. They are the supreme arbiters of the fate of their armies and wield visionary powers far in excess of those ever granted to a general in the field. Various methods have been evolved to overcome this inherent weakness, but most war-gamers consider that it cannot be completely eliminated and many would not wish it to be.

There is one rule, however, which is widely accepted and does to an extent limit the powers of the players. It concerns **vision**. If opposing troops cannot see each other, it is highly unlikely that they will make counter preparations. This type of reaction is, therefore, generally prohibited unless troops are within one another's line of vision. Likewise, nineteenth-century artillery could not normally fire upon a target unless it was visible, and rules limiting vision allow troops to hide with immunity behind woods or rises in the ground. Natur-ally, modern artillery techniques and communications severely restrict the effect of this rule in twentieth-century conflicts.

When determining line of vision, it is important to remem-ber that the vertical figure scale normally bears no relationship whatsoever to the horizontal scale. The line of vision must relate to the ground scale, which really means that it should be taken from and to the figures' bases, details of this principle, of course, depending upon the ground scale employed in the game.

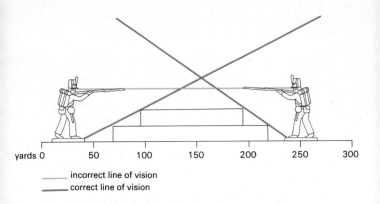

____ incorrect line of vision
▬▬▬ correct line of vision

Line of vision. Using 20mm figures and a ground scale of 1 inch to 50 yards, the figures represent a height of some 150 feet. However, their line of vision should be taken from a point about five feet above the ground. For the sake of convenience, the top of a figure's base is usually treated as 'eye level'. Using this principle, the two soldiers shown cannot see each other from their respective sides of the hill.

Another widely practised rule which is intended to limit the players' powers of reaction calls for orders to be written at the start of each move. The players then move the various units to conform with these directions.

Rules also govern the **time/space ratio**. If wargaming is to be at all realistic, there must be a relationship between time and space, or distance, and the correct calculation of these factors is of paramount importance to the whole of game structure.

Time is expressed by the move. The move represents a given time – one minute, one hour, or whatever is required. During the move, the figures can march so many yards or miles, fire their guns so many times, and so on. Thus time, as expressed by a move, dictates the capabilities of every piece upon the wargame table. Space, as previously explained, is governed by a scale which is common to both the area occupied by the figures and the terrain. Therefore all movement and weapon ranges are mathematically determined by time and space scales.

The long weapon-ranges in modern warfare are inconvenient for the average table top, and some players use a space scale which is completely different from that noted in the terrain section. In this scale, distance is coupled to a graph with an ascending curve. The further away from the focal point one goes, the sharper becomes the rise in the curve of the graph. At 2 inches, opposing figures may be considered to be 50 yards apart, but at 36 inches, the distance may be 3 miles. Time is represented in the conventional way. This system has the advantage of allowing supporting artillery to be present on the same wargame layout as the forward infantry.

Once the basic time/space concept is accepted, the degree of realism is entirely dependent upon the wargamer's mathematics and his research into every aspect of warfare in his chosen period. It is not enough to know that the maximum effective range of an aimed musket was 175 yards. He also needs to know its rapidity of fire and its effect at lesser distances. Likewise, knowledge of the ordinary marching speed of a foot soldier is insufficient since, in the time allotted to a move, the soldier in question may be ordered to undertake some complicated manoeuvre – such as forming a square, unlimbering a gun, or building a pontoon bridge. All of these activities must be accurately related to the time scale. In waging modern campaigns it is also necessary to evaluate vehicle performance.

All **movement** has to be controlled by rules. Infantry moves fall into two classes. Individual moves are elastic, including loose warfare such as skirmishing during the Napoleonic and American Civil Wars or by all infantrymen during the Second World War. Group movement rules cover the bulk of infantry movement during the classic horse-foot-and-gun period and they are of extreme importance during the Napoleonic Wars. Apart from the then relatively new tactic of skirmishing, the security of Napoleonic fighting formations depended upon their cohesion. Battalions of infantry acted as an entity, and it is necessary to discover how they manoeuvred and fought before this type of warfare can be interpreted by rules. The drill and tactics of different armies varied widely and, ideally, rules should reflect this.

When a unit changes formation, say from a square into a line, the time factor should be calculated and expressed in terms of a move. A successful way of doing this is to break the move down into ten or fifteen parts and then to equate the various stages of the movement with these subdivisions. This system has the advantage of enabling the figures to perform several functions instead of just one. The loading and discharge of firearms, issuing of orders, formation changes, and other time-consuming activities can all be catered for in this way.

Movement is governed by the time and ground scales. Using the regulation movements of the Union Army during the American Civil War, the distances shown could be covered in one minute. A ground scale of 1 inch to 50 yards has been chosen for this example. A 'charge' was executed only in the final stages of an attack and lasted for some fifteen seconds.

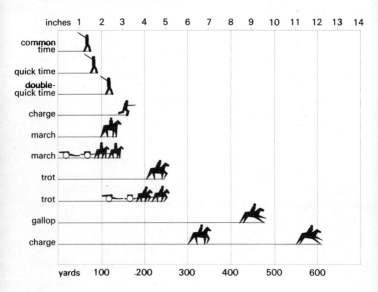

Movement should also reflect three other factors. Firstly, infantry, cavalry, mechanized troops, and heavy wagons were all capable of different speeds of manoeuvre. Secondly, many of these classes were able to operate at different paces. Cavalry, for instance, could walk, trot, canter, or gallop. Likewise, the modern infantryman can perform a variety of movements, ranging from crawling to running, which again call for a variety of speeds. Thirdly, the nature of terrain and even weather conditions affect movement speeds. Time should be allowed for troops to surmount such obstacles as walls and narrow streams. Natural features such as woods, marshes, and ploughed fields will also slow down movement, and mud will cause further delay. One only has to look at the delays sustained by both Napoleon's and Hitler's forces in the East to be aware of the effect of mud.

The extent to which moves should be penalized for obstacles crossed depends on what is taken to be the basic move. If the 'average' move is gauged as being made on firm ground, such as a fairly flat field, one must give bonuses for movement on metalled roads. It is, however, quite convenient to take the average as a road move and to penalize a unit as soon as it moves away from a well-made highway.

When moving along a road, the width of the road should be taken into account: troops that are mounted upon unit bases will have a frontage considerably in excess of the road width. The unit depth becomes the frontage, and if the sub-units are strung out one behind another a fairly accurate representation of a column of route is obtained. If the unit concerned is not mounted in this way, its length in column of route must be ascertained and space must be left on the road accordingly.

The movement rules of a modern campaign can be extremely complicated. Many different types and makes of vehicle must be taken into consideration, as well as most of the factors noted already. For the purposes of general movement, vehicles should be governed not so much by their capabilities as by the speeds imposed upon them by movement discipline. There will, however, always be that moment when a driver wishes to use the maximum power at his disposal and provision for this must be made.

Many wargamers, as noted earlier, adopt the rule of writing

all orders down at the start of each move to bring wargaming one step closer to reality. As a further refinement of this concept, the players need write orders to only a relatively small number of brigades or divisions within an army. This idea is based on the premise that the players have written the rules around the drill and tactics of the appropriate period. Thus, once a particular unit has been ordered to undertake a series of tasks, the whole operation continues, as dictated by the movement regulations of the period, until its conclusion, perhaps five or eight moves later.

In all periods **firepower** and its effect can be expressed in mathematical terms, but it is often difficult to gather sufficient information on which to base calculations. Weapon range is naturally linked to ground scale. If, for example, a ground scale of 1 inch to 25 yards is adopted, then the maximum effective musket range of 175 yards becomes 7 inches. It is, of course, essential to know the range details of weapons, and

French dragoons on the march. Alternately riding and walking, a speed of some $3\frac{3}{4}$ to $4\frac{1}{4}$mph could easily be maintained.

this can call for extensive research into the subject, especially where modern warfare is concerned, since the variety of weapons is so large and sophisticated.

Having determined weapon range, it is then necessary to evaluate weapon effect, and this is certainly one of the most complex problems that a wargamer must face. Distance from target, rapidity of fire, and actual effect must be related to each other before casualties can be assessed.

Distance from target presents no problem since this is easily gauged by the space between the weapon and the target on the wargame table. With visually-aimed weapons, an increase in range generally entails a decrease in effectiveness. This is not necessarily the case when one considers heavy weaponry which is aimed indirectly.

Rapidity of fire is important because of the time scale of the game. If, for example, a move is taken as being $2\frac{1}{2}$ minutes, a player must know how many times a weapon can fire during

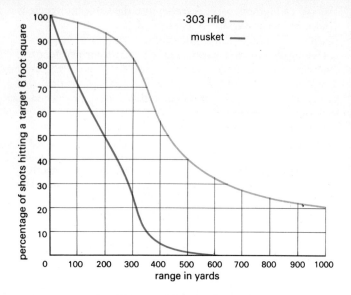

Comparisons of the efficiency of Napoleonic and Second World War weapons: (*above*) a French musket and a British rifle and (*opposite*) field artillery.

that period. Rapidity of fire in this context means the number of times that a weapon can be effectively discharged and bears no relationship whatsoever to the rpm (rounds per minute) statistic of modern automatic weapons, which is a theoretical rate of fire obtainable by the mechanism, but which, in fact, would destroy the weapon in a short space of time if employed in the field.

Given that rate of fire and range can be calculated as described, actual effect is still difficult to calculate because of other unknown factors such as the proficiency of the weapon user and target movement.

Weapon proficiency can be linked to a system of troop grading. Many wargamers include in their armies units designated 'élite'. The purpose of this is to represent the difference in quality between such units as Napoleon's Old Guard and fresh conscript infantry straight from the training

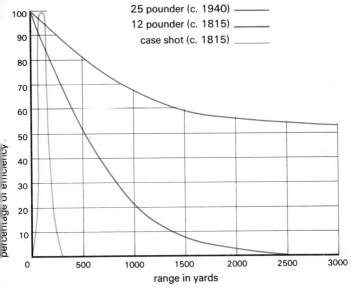

Both the graphs on this spread are based on a single shot; the efficiency of the 1939–45 weapons is much greater if one considers their rapidity of fire.

depots. If one accepts the line infantryman as the average, then fire rules can incorporate a bonus effect when veteran or élite troops use their weapons. Likewise, units below average – such as the Prussian *Landwehr* in 1813, militia, and reservists – can be penalized.

Another factor which detracts from the effectiveness of firepower is 'cover'. This is a term to indicate features behind which a soldier may shelter. Soft cover – vegetation – is effective since it confuses the aim of a weapon user. Hard cover – masonry or earthworks – is of value since it actively protects anyone who happens to be sheltering in or behind it.

Troop formation also has an effect on firepower. A dense, or large, formation was a target which could easily be hit. The weight and velocity of a cannon ball would plough through as many men as were standing in its path. French columns were particularly vulnerable since they were twenty-four ranks deep. In contrast, the loose-combat tactics of modern warfare lessen the chance of injury or death.

Even weather plays a part in weapon efficiency. Flintlock weapons could be rendered useless by a heavy downpour, and mud retarded round-shot by reducing its ricochet range. Modern shells with impact fuses are most effective when they hit a hard surface – ground that has been frozen or baked solid – since they have no opportunity to bury themselves before exploding, as would occur in damp ground or mud.

The solution to the whole problem of fire effect is to gather sufficient factual information to create a statistical basis upon which to work. Given, however, that the effects of firepower

The German 'Panzerfaust'. Modern weapon technology has produced simple equipment of tremendous power.

can be assessed, they must then be equated to the figures on the wargame table. If, as is usual, it is necessary to adopt a figure scale, then the fact that an odd soldier here or there is disabled counts for very little. Single casualties can be counted up and, when a number equal to the game figure scale has been accumulated, a figure can be removed. However, effective unit strengths can be kept as a running total and there is no real need to remove a single figure. If, as may be the case with modern warfare, a one to one scale is adopted, then obviously the single casualty has great importance and should be removed immediately.

Firepower has one important effect other than the physical. Most wargamers would agree that the psychological effect of being fired upon is more important than the number of casualties that occur. **Morale** is, perhaps, the most crucial factor in warfare. It may be defined as the will to win, a mental force which determines the limit of a soldier's or an army's endurance. The character of the commander, the losses sustained, patriotism, comfort, the chance of success, or the certainty of defeat, these and many more factors influence morale. The morale of an army can be completely unpredictable. It can drop from high to low in an incredibly short space of time, or it can remain high against all odds. The French Army at Waterloo disintegrated and fled from the battlefield upon seeing Napoleon's final attack defeated, but at the same time, with defeat all around them, the Old Guard formed square and tried to cover the flight of the Army.

Few facts are constant when considering morale in the wider sense, but at a lower level there are certain elements which tend to work toward either high or low morale. It would seem that if troops view their own chance of success favourably their morale will remain high; reduce this confidence and, in all probability, morale will drop. Thus, factors such as the strength of a position, the availability of supports or reliefs, the amount of opposition encountered, the percentage of casualties, and success or failure themselves have a direct effect on morale.

Morale can break at any time, but it happens most often in a crisis. The point in battle when morale most commonly fails is the moment before hand-to-hand fighting. It is for precisely this reason that such combat was extremely rare. The morale of one side would break before that of the other, with the inevitable result that one side literally ran away, leaving the field to, or being pursued by, the victor. Another consistent result of morale failure was that the formation which broke suffered by far the highest number of casualties, despite the fact that up to the moment of breaking there was probably no marked disproportion between them. When broken troops retired or were driven in defeat from an action, they were thinking only of saving themselves, whilst the victor was still intent upon destroying an opponent.

At the best of times, morale was, and is, open to question and there can be no hard and fast rules governing it. The wargamer is, therefore, forced to adopt some method of chance to simulate the morale of his armies. Dice generally provide this element. Each unit can be given a basic morale value which can be added to, or subtracted from, depending upon circumstances. Thus, well-led troops in a strongly entrenched position who are well supported at their rear and on their

Spanish infantry, c. 1812. Troops decisively broken in combat would invariably leave the battlefield as a disordered mob.

flanks will improve their basic morale value, whilst their opponents, who have advanced at grievous loss to themselves across open ground through heavy artillery, musket, or machine-gun fire, will have their morale value decreased.

The question of whether one side or the other will panic and retreat can then be assessed by simple mathematics based upon the number of troops involved, their respective morale values, and a dice throw. This calculation includes the number of troops since it is logical to assume that the larger side will stand a better chance of winning. Both head counts are multiplied by the result of a dice throw, with the morale values being assessed as either additions to, or subtractions from, the number thrown on the dice. In the example quoted, it would seem fairly certain that the attackers would be defeated, but there exists an outside chance that they might win and reverse the expected outcome, as happens so often upon the battlefield.

If the morale of both sides holds, then hand-to-hand combat ensues, and this is generally known as the mêlée. The mêlée

is a device intended to consume time and to remove a small number of combatants from the table. Its outcome is decided by another morale calculation at the end of the move, or perhaps in that following.

The mêlée, and indeed all situations in which morale plays some part, must take account of the differences between the various grades of troops that compose armies. Apart from the obvious branch distinctions – such as heavy and light cavalry, and infantry – and in the modern period the differences derived from armament, tanks, machine guns and so on, provision for élite troops can be made. These units can be given a value, in addition to the weapon-proficiency bonus already mentioned, and this is then added to their morale value. Thus resolution, better training, or whatever it is that sets them apart, is recognized. Likewise, there is no reason why a lower morale value could not be ascribed to second-line troops.

ADVANCED WARGAMES

Advanced wargames are a logical development from the basic game. Once an ordinary wargame has been evolved and found to be satisfactory, it is only natural that the players should want to develop it. The first step is simply to elaborate the rules, incorporating features which were not included in the initial game concept. Ammunition supply, signal networks, and a command structure are examples of refinements that can be added to the basic wargame.

Logistics

Logistics, or the organizing of supplies, is a factor which can be included in advanced wargaming. It really makes little difference to the actual play if this element is excluded, but some wargamers feel that if the object of wargaming is to re-create warfare, then no game is complete without it. Certainly the supply factor can significantly effect the outcome of a siege because it then assumes an importance which it does not have in a normal encounter. What is actually comprised in the term logistics is also a question for debate among wargamers.

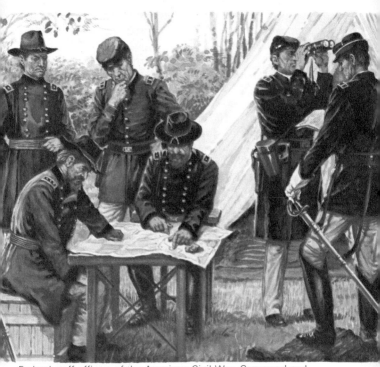

Federal staff officers of the American Civil War. Command and communication structures are important in advanced wargaming.

Some argue that munitions are all that is really required since troops can live off the country; others insist that rations are equally important. The answer lies, however, somewhere between the two.

No army can fight if it is not provided with powder and shot, and the quantity that it consumes relates directly to events on the wargame table. The amount of ammunition each unit has can be recorded and continually updated, but this can become a lengthy book-keeping exercise. Alternatively, ammunition tokens can be given to each unit, and for each move in which the unit is engaged in a fire fight one token is removed. Replenishment is achieved by munition columns arriving with fresh supplies. Food and forage are not as important as munitions, but they are, none the less, significant. It may even be decided to penalize the morale of troops with empty stomachs!

The logistical problems of a modern army are potentially even more complicated than those of any period campaign. There is, after all, the additional diversity of ammunition types and the question of fuel for petrol and diesel-driven vehicles. All can be obtained only from depots by a large supply and transport system. This again leads to an almost unlimited amount of book-keeping. If the supply factor is taken to its logical conclusion, the administrative tail of an army becomes larger than its head, as indeed has happened.

A Union supply column at the time of the American Civil War.
Most advanced games take account of supply and reinforcement.

Campaigns

The next step in wargaming requires that the players cease to think of a wargame as an isolated encounter and see it instead as an integral part of a campaign. One of the advantages of playing a campaign is that the object of battles, instead of being rather doubtful as in a single encounter, can be seen with absolute clarity. To this end, it is necessary to provide a purpose for the campaign.

Campaigns are best played on maps. Each side can be given a town which represents its capital, centre of power, or base depot. To capture the town so designated would be a simple object. However, there can be more than one centre of power for each side. In fact, entire countries can be drawn up with their principle towns, depots, and, if required, fortresses, or lines of fortification. Each side arranges its forces upon the map and then movement begins in much the same way as on a wargame table with due regard to the time/space scale.

Some wargamers use three identical maps for the actual campaign moves. Each player has a map on which to plot the moves of his forces whilst a master map is controlled by an umpire who uses markers to represent the movement of both sides and can inform the players when contact is made. A wargame table is then laid out to represent the map at the point of contact, and the troops involved appear on the table, conforming to their map moves. Game moves must relate to the broader campaign moves on the map, but there will be perhaps five moves on the table top to one on a map, thus filling in the detail of an encounter. Reinforcements, for example, can advance towards the sound of the guns and appear at different points in the game. This type of game structure allows for conflicts of all sizes, from outpost skirmishes to full-scale battles, and sets them within a meaningful context.

The circumstances of a battle dictate when an action should cease. In an unrelated encounter there is a tendency to fight to the bitter end, but within the context of a campaign it usually becomes obvious to one side that a point has been reached beyond which it would be foolish to fight.

Reconnaissance is important in all campaigns but particularly when an umpire is coordinating troop contacts and the players are moving their pieces without knowledge of the enemy. Numerous small mobile patrols ahead of the main forces can provide intelligence, but these patrols generally encounter similar opposition and much minor skirmishing takes place before one side or the other gains the advantage of knowing the enemy dispositions and movements. Operations of this nature provide a realistic role for light cavalry and reconnaissance troops which is absent in a basic wargame.

Once intelligence is gathered, a system of communications becomes important. In modern campaigns, this is achieved simply by allowing for radio networks, but in any pre-radio period the job of passing vital information devolves upon mounted couriers. Not until the messenger has actually reported to headquarters can the umpire inform a player of what his forward troops have seen. Movement orders must be conveyed by the same method. In such periods as the American Civil War, the rules must provide for the existence of the telegraph. Signal troops can lay line and, assuming that a message is delivered at a telegraph office, it can then be speedily communicated to its destination.

Railways can play an important part in a campaign. During the latter part of the nineteenth century and up to the First World War, they were the principle method by which mass movement of troops was accomplished. It therefore becomes necessary to stipulate the size and capacity of any railway system in the game. The existence of railways also gives more scope to the engineer services. These are absolutely essential in a campaign, bridging, fortifications, and demolitions all requiring their expert attention.

Armies undertaking campaigns must also have realistic medical services. Casualties should contain a very high proportion of wounded and, since there is no way of telling how long a campaign may last, there is a good chance that troops injured in the early stages may be returned for duty later. It is therefore desirable to have sufficient ambulances available to transport at least lightly wounded troops, since to leave them may mean that they become prisoners of war.

Incidentally, in a realistic wargame provision must be made for prisoners of war. When they are taken in battle, it becomes necessary to escort them to the rear, and, if large numbers of prisoners are taken, permanent camps must be set up to house them and troops have to be detailed for guard duty. The latter calls either for the detachment of troops from the field army or provides a role for military police. The advantage in having

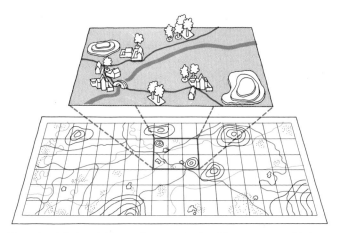

The role of the model layout in campaigning. The wargame table is set out in accordance with the geographical features of the area in which opposing forces have come into contact.

numerous prisoners of war is that they can be set to work repairing damaged bridges, roads, or railway tracks, which relieves the strain on the captor's engineering service. A study of the history of warfare reveals how often captives were induced to change sides and this point may well appeal to many wargamers.

Political and economic wargames
War and politics are inseparably linked and this fact provides the logic for political wargames. The political game gives the campaign its correct setting just as the campaign gave a context to table-top battles.

The only requirement for political wargaming is that there must be more than two players; six or eight is the number normally involved, but there is no reason why there should not be twenty or thirty players. Each player is in control of a 'country' which has its own armed forces. The strength of each state can vary depending upon its geographic location; some may have large armies, others with a coastline may have naval power. The armies, fleets, and air forces at the disposal of each player must be determined at the start of a game. When a large number of players are involved, it is useful to have countries of varying might. The most enthusiastic players can take the larger powers, whilst minor states can be given to those who do not expect to have time for complete involvement in the game.

A time scale must be provided, one actual day or session equalling a week or month of game time; this scale in turn relates to the time scale on the wargame table or map board. It is not necessary to maintain the political time-scale with complete accuracy since time can be very easily made up if it begins to fall into arrears. However, time lapses should not disrupt events which have already happened – something which could easily occur with a large number of participants, some of whom may be playing in near isolation.

Game mechanics are very simple. The players make alliances and then the power blocs commence map campaigns and table-top battles. Since each player is his own master, he is quite at liberty to deceive, betray, and lie to his own advantage, and the political map of the area involved is usually subject to frequent change. This system can produce almost any kind of political situation – two or more power blocs, neutrals, even no hostility at all; it also provides excellent objectives for military and naval undertakings and for political machinations which are interesting in their own right and which, if governed by further rules, can simulate those of a given period and situation.

No country is any stronger than its economy allows, and an economic element can be introduced into campaigning or political wargaming, but it is only of value when it is used in a game that covers a considerable period of time.

As with political wargaming, players are allotted countries; then they are given populations, industries, raw materials, and so on. Each player can then mobilize his or her entire country, distributing the population between industry and the armed forces. Industry commences to arm and equip army, navy, and air force, and the wargame starts. Each national economy is utilized to support its armed forces in the field, replace losses of men and materials, and create additional power as required. It is up to the player to decide how best to use his industry. There will inevitably come a point at which a country's resources are stretched to the limit and it is then that the choice must be made either to maintain production or to enlarge the forces in the field.

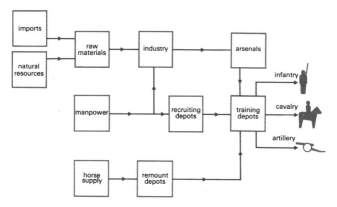

This chart illustrates a simple economic game. In time of war manpower and materials are related to form a basis for industrial production, and the surplus population and the armaments manufactured furnish the army.

The flow of raw materials can be another interesting aspect of an economic game. Certain key materials could be denied to certain countries, thus forcing an element of trade into the game and creating alliances based upon economic necessity. Transport systems are also required to move raw materials from their source to the factories, and the finished products from factory to front.

Economic games offer a vast scope to the wargamer and to achieve realism it is necessary to undertake research into the spheres of industry and economics. This type of game is more interesting, and much more complex, if it is set in a modern period, where it is possible to subject a country to strategic bombing, but it can be applied to any period.

Research for wargaming

So far I have detailed many of the methods by which one can construct a wargame. In the final analysis, however, all wargames should be founded upon historical fact. It therefore follows that much of the wargamer's energy must be expended in the quest for accurate data with which to modify and perfect his original game.

No single source will provide all of the details that are required by the wargamer, and he is thus forced to plough through many volumes, extracting the relevant facts as he goes along. This information should be carefully accumulated in notebooks or on index cards; a true understanding of the facts that have been collected often rests upon the way in which they are compiled.

The problems of research extend even further. Even after many years, it is possible – indeed it is almost certain – that numerous essential facts will still not have been discovered. Another problem that will be encountered is that of misleading or inaccurate information and, ideally, it is always best to check facts against a second source. However, one must also be aware of the possibility that once an obscure and incorrect point is committed to print it will be followed by other authors and in this way become regarded as the truth.

As far as is possible, research should be conducted through publications contemporary to the subjects that they cover. On pages 124–5 is a brief bibliography relating to the three periods covered in the second part of this volume. Many of the publications noted have bibliographic lists which provide the reader with additional information on source material.

Despite the great variety of periods to which wargaming can be applied, the following chapters provide basic information on just three of them. The choice of these periods has been determined by their widespread popularity. Whilst it would be foolish to claim that the following pages give all of the information required by the wargamer, it can, none the less, be fairly stated that this data is sufficient to provide a sound framework upon which to build factually accurate games.

A Napoleonic battlefield, typical in that it is dominated by a
geographically strong position and shows troops manoeuvring in mass

THE NAPOLEONIC WARS

The Napoleonic Wars lasted from 1805 until 1815, and during
that period all of Europe was involved, at one time or another.
By 1811, most of the continent was under French domination,
but after that year Napoleon's armies suffered a series of
reverses which culminated in his abdication in early 1814.
The final phase of the Wars included Napoleon's return from
exile, his defeat at Waterloo, and his banishment to the island
of St Helena in 1815.

During the Wars France fought the following campaigns
(dates and main adversaries listed): 1805, Austria and Russia;
1806, Prussia; 1807, Russia; 1809, Austria; 1812, Russia;
1813 and 1814 Austria, Russia, Prussia, and Sweden; and
1815, Great Britain and Prussia. In addition, the British fought

in the Peninsular War, the most protracted encounter of the period, 1807–14.

Firepower

The basic infantry weapon was a musket, and, although several types were in use with the various armies, there was little difference between them in performance. A series of tests conducted by the Prussians against a target 6 feet high and 100 feet long produced the following results: at 85 yards about seventy per cent of the musket balls fired hit the target; at 170 yards this figure had fallen to fifty per cent; and at 350 yards to twenty-five per cent. Above this range, the number of hits fell off rapidly until at 500 yards only one per cent were striking the target. The target represented a line of

Napoleonic weapons: a Prussian 6-pounder cannon (A); a Prussian cavalry pistol (B); a French musket (C); a British Baker rifle (D); an Austrian *Jäger* rifle (E); an Austrian cavalry pistol (F); and a French 8-pounder cannon (G).

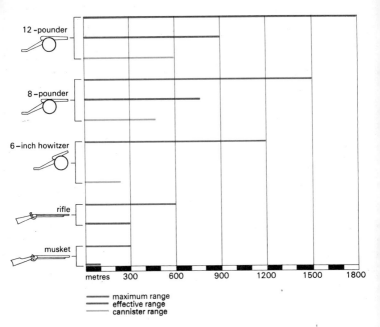

12-pounder

8-pounder

6-inch howitzer

rifle

musket

metres 300 600 900 1200 1500 1800

maximum range
effective range
cannister range

A comparison of Napoleonic weapon ranges

infantry, and under 'real' conditions many of the strikes would have been ineffective since they would have passed between soldiers without actually hitting them. It should also be noted that these tests were conducted under ideal circumstances, such as were not usually found on a battlefield.

Some special light-infantry units or individuals were armed with a short rifle. Rifling in the barrel makes a weapon more accurate, and at 350 yards, for instance, the Prussian *Jäger* rifle was four times more effective than the musket.

What really distinguished the fire effect of the infantry from one army to another was the weapon proficiency of the individual soldiers. In the Prussian Army it was reckoned that a musket could be loaded and fired in 45 seconds, which was well below the British standard of two, or even three, times per minute. In the French Army little attention was given to musket training, and in 1813 it was even normal for conscripts to fire a musket only two or three times before they went into action. This undervaluing of infantry fire-power is also demonstrated by the fact that the French were alone in not adopting a rifle for their skirmishers.

One other factor affected infantry firepower: after some fifteen or twenty discharges the black-powder used as a propellent fouled the musket barrel, making it more difficult to load the weapon. With a rifle, slow loading was always a problem because the round had to be hammered down the barrel owing to its tight fit.

Two types of artillery pieces were used by the various armies: cannon and howitzers. Cannon employed direct fire whereas the howitzer used a high trajectory so that its missile would land on top of the target, this being particularly useful against buildings. Cannon mostly fired solid metal spheres, i.e cannon balls, but with a howitzer it was possible to dis-charge a round containing a bursting charge which was fitted with a simple time-fuse lit by hand before the weapon was fired. Artillery could also use canister or case shot. This type of ammunition consisted of numerous musket balls in a thin casing. When the piece was fired, the musket balls spread

French horse artillery. The pieces were light enough for the gun teams to keep up with the cavalry.

from the muzzle of the cannon or howitzer and caused considerable harm to any troops that were unfortunate enough to be caught in the resulting arc.

Cannon were designated by the weight of shot they fired. In the French service were pieces firing 4-, 6-, 8-, and 12-pound balls, their maximum range being 1,200, 1,250, 1,500, and 1,800 metres respectively. Ricochet increased these ranges still further, each bound theoretically being equal to fifty per cent of the preceding one. The French 6-inch howitzer had a maximum range of 1,200 metres. Effective range of all pieces was considered to be about fifty per cent of the maximum. Canister range was about thirty-three per cent of the maximum range of a cannon and about sixteen per cent in the case of a howitzer. Owing to the shortness and large calibre of a howitzer barrel, the arc of spread was much greater than that of a cannon, which made it a very effective weapon at short range.

Tactics

These varied from army to army, but so great was the impact of the French Revolutionary and Imperial Armies on contemporary military thought that by 1812 all countries except Britain had adopted modified forms of the French columnar system.

To be effective, the old linear formations had required long-service regular soldiers, and, although by 1805 the French Army was of sufficient quality to operate a mixed columnar and linear system of tactics, after about 1808 the troops were less and less competent and the importance of the column rose in consequence.

The French reasoned that the old linear formations were of use only in the fire fight, where they allowed the maximum number of muskets to be aimed at the enemy. For purposes of manoeuvre they adopted the column. Theoretically, the column advanced rapidly until, reaching the enemy, it had the choice of either charging or changing into a line to begin firing. To cover the column whilst it advanced, skirmishers were thrown out to keep enemy soldiers at bay and to prevent them from damaging the main body of troops until the column was either in a position to use its weight in an attack or had deployed into line. The skirmishers were an essential part of the scheme since, without their effective cooperation, a column could be delayed, dispirited, and even disrupted by fire before it had reached its objective. At times the skirmishers were so strong that they forced battlelines to withdraw, without assistance from supporting troops.

The column was based on a battalion; its six companies could be drawn up either one behind another – the 'column of companies' – or two wide and three deep – the 'column of division'. Each company was three men deep. These battalion columns could be joined into giant columns, as at Wagram in 1809, when no less than twenty-three battalions were thus deployed. Each battalion had a company of voltigeurs which formed the skirmishing line.

Only the British Army placed its reliance upon the line, although in fact it changed the traditional three-deep line to one which was only two-deep; in a fire fight, the third man could not fire his musket and was therefore wasted. It was this two-deep firing line that met and defeated the column

A French infantry column advancing on English skirmishers

in the Peninsular War and at Waterloo, but only because of two other factors. Firstly, it was realized that a skirmishing line was required to drive away the French voltigeurs and to attack the column before it reached the British line. Thus, in the Peninsular, the skirmishers of the British Army were gradually increased until, by 1812, they completely over-powered the French voltigeurs. The result was to subject the French columns to a fire for which they were never intended. Secondly, the British line was always on the reverse side of a ridge, a stratagem which compelled the French to launch their attacks in ignorance of the true British positions.

The column, however, had one decided advantage over the line as a battlefield formation – it was nowhere near as vulnerable to cavalry. By closing the ranks and filling the gaps between the companies, a column of division could be converted into a close square in a matter of seconds. With a line, it was a protracted manoeuvre to form square, and there were numerous incidents throughout the Peninsular War and the Waterloo campaign when the British infantry was caught in a

line formation by French cavalry and suffered grievously. The classic English square was hollow and each wall was formed by four ranks of infantrymen, the front rank kneeling and presenting their bayonets to the attacking horsemen. There was very little chance of cavalry breaking a formed square, and during the whole of the Peninsular War only two such instances occurred.

Cavalry tactics were also dominated by the concept of mass. Squadron columns, either one behind another or in echelon, were much favoured. The grand cavalry attacks of the French Army consisted of numerous squadron and regimental columns joined together into one giant formation, in much the same way as the infantry at Wagram. There was, however, a

Napoleonic tactical formations: a column of divisions (fig. 1); a column of companies (fig. 2); and squares placed so as not to fire upon each other (fig. 3).

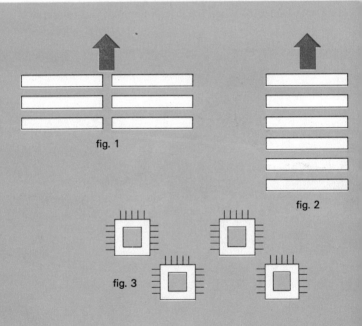

place for the line, and formation very much depended upon requirements. In small cavalry engagements the use of line was quite common.

The mounted troops most commonly used on the battle-field were the so-called 'heavy' cavalry – large men on big horses. The 'light' cavalry, the hussars, light dragoons, and chasseurs, were primarily used for outpost work. It was they who scouted ahead of the main army, pursued the enemy, and provided the numerous small mounted details required by an army.

Some armies employed mounted skirmishers. These advanced at some distance before the main body and their role was similar to that of their infantry counterparts. They were conspicuously absent in the French Army.

All armies had foot and horse artillery. The former consisted of the medium and heavy pieces, which were transported at marching pace, whereas the latter could accompany the cavalry and had light guns with ample teams and mounted gunners.

Foot artillery tended to operate according to rigid principles since, once a battle began, it could not be quickly transported to a new position. It was usually drawn up in advance of the main battleline by the French, who generally deployed their forces in an aggressive posture, and placed close to the line in the case of the British. The proximity of artillery to infantry was never liked by the latter since the guns drew fire and, inevitably, offered a better target to the enemy's artillerymen.

Horse artillery, owing to its mobility, had a completely different role. It was intended to be at the decisive point at the right moment, and this is borne out by a study of Napoleonic military history. Ideally, the horse artillery would accompany an attacking force so that when enemy defences were seen to be strong the guns could be called forward to weaken them in preparation for the infantry or cavalry attack. This was especially useful when the guns were in the company of cavalry that was attacking infantry. The infantry would form square to resist cavalry, the cavalry would draw off, and the artillery would hammer away at the square, which was pinned in position for fear of being attacked by horsemen should it try to move.

French voltigeurs formed the skirmishing lines of the French Army.

The French Army

The army which took the field towards the end of the Empire differed considerably from Napoleon's army of 1805. By 1813 its organization and uniforms had changed and its quality had greatly deteriorated.

The infantry were formed into line and light regiments. The light infantry had been the troops that provided the dense skirmishing lines of the Republic, but under Napoleon their special tactical role largely disappeared. Infantry regiments were divided into battalions, normally three, but in 1812 certain regiments sent up to five battalions to Russia, some acting as complete brigades. One battalion was always held in France as a regimental depot, supplying replacements to those in the field. The battalion was divided into eight companies, but in 1808 this was reduced to six, four of which were centre companies and two élite. The centre companies in a line regiment were designated fusiliers, and the élite companies, grenadiers and voltigeurs. In the light regiments, chasseurs took the place of the fusiliers and carbineers that of the grenadiers.

Infantry battalions had a full establishment of about one thousand men, but in practice seldom exceeded seven hundred.

The French heavy cavalry consisted of regiments of cuirassiers and carbineers, and, together with some of the dragoon regiments, formed the reserve cavalry, which was always held intact for major battle attacks. The light cavalry was comprised of hussars, chasseurs, and, after 1811, lancers. Cavalry regiments numbered about one thousand men divided into four squadrons. As with the infantry, the full establishment was seldom fielded, and after 1812 there was a crippling shortage of horses which reduced many regiments to the strength of only one squadron.

The artillery was organized into foot and horse companies, the former handling the heavier pieces and the latter the light. Each company comprised six cannon and two howitzers: this mixing of pieces was common during the Napoleonic period.

Apart from the forces already noted, there was Napoleon's Guard, which by 1813 had become a small army in its own right with all branches of the service being represented. The Old Guard was relatively small and consisted of the senior infantry and cavalry regiments. The so-called Middle Guard contained only the two fusilier regiments, and the Young Guard, which was recruited mainly after 1809, contained numerous regiments of voltigeurs and tuirailleurs. The titles of these units were merely complementary and had no relation to their tactical role.

Infantry regiments were grouped in twos or threes to form brigades, which in turn were similarly joined with an additional complement of artillery to form divisions. An army corps consisted of a number of divisions, this depending upon the importance attached to its role in battle. In the early wars of the Empire, it was usually two or three, but by 1812 there was a marked difference in size, some having as many as five or six divisions. Each corps was given a complement of artillery, cavalry, and other supporting troops, thus becoming a complete army in itself. The reserve cavalry constituted an entire corps but it had grown so large by 1812 that it was split into a number of cavalry corps in the following year. However, each corps was scarcely stronger than an earlier division.

Reference has already been made to columnar tactics, but certain aspects of French tactical doctrine have not been mentioned. When holding a position, the French Army would generally adopt a formation that was known as the 'mixed order'. This was the name given to a battleline formed with its flanks resting upon heavy columns. It was generally achieved by forming alternate battalions into columns and lines, and it had the advantages of the column's weight and stability in defence, together with the firepower of the line. Because the

French soldiers of the Napoleonic Wars. (*Left to right*) a corporal of line grenadiers, 1812–15; a sergeant of foot grenadiers, Imperial Guard; a chasseur, 10th Light Infantry; a fusilier, 1806–7; a fusilier in campaign dress, 1813–14; a cuirassier, 9th Regiment; a hussar, 11th Regiment; a lancer, 5th Regiment; a lancer of the Guard, 2nd Regiment; and a *chasseur à cheval* of the Guard.

flanks of the line were always anchored upon columns, it was less susceptible to a cavalry attack. The mixed order is reputed to have been much favoured by Napoleon and there were instances of it being used for attack.

Another feature of French tactics was that in most of the major battles Napoleon's reserve artillery formed huge batteries which were intended to decimate the enemy's line at a selected point in preparation for a massed columnar assault. To this end, he generally held back the bulk of his 12-pounder foot-artillery companies, together with the heavy cavalry, as part of the army reserve to be deployed at his discretion. The object of having a large reserve of heavy cavalry with the main field army was that it could be launched when the enemy was seen to be wavering after a massed infantry assault. If used correctly, this mass of horsemen was a victory-winning weapon.

The British Army

The British foot troops throughout the period were a well-trained, steady, and reliable force, probably the best infantry in Europe at the time. They were organized into battalions and administered on a regimental basis, but it was seldom that two battalions of the same regiment fought alongside each other. The battalion contained eight centre companies and two flanking companies, light and grenadier. A complete battalion numbered a little over one thousand men. The light companies acted as skirmishing troops. British infantry brigades consisted of some four or five battalions and two brigades generally formed a division. In addition to the line regiments, there were rifle battalions, which were distributed by companies throughout the army. The Anglo-Portuguese divisions in the Peninsula contained two rifle companies and a complete battalion of Portuguese cacadores, which were used to strengthen the skirmishing line; with these additions the line was strong enough to counter the most vigorous of French skirmishers.

The British cavalry was a competent force with a tendency to impetuosity. Several instances occurred of British horsemen riding to destruction because they could not be kept in hand. Cavalry regiments seldom fielded an effective strength of more than four hundred men. Three or four regiments formed a brigade and the brigades were either held together under a central command or distributed throughout the army as circumstances required.

The artillery was divided into horse artillery and foot batteries, each equipped with six pieces. An innovation used by the Royal Horse Artillery was the rocket. Launched from a small portable ramp, it had a bursting charge and was designed to explode at the end of its flight. The main value of this novel weapon was that it created considerable consternation in the French ranks and caused many horses to bolt, thus making it much more effective than its limited capability warranted. There were rocket units at Leipzig in 1813 and at the Battle of Waterloo.

A British square, formed from the 30th and 73rd Regiments, 1815. The mixing of units was uncommon, but there is evidence that it did occur at Waterloo.

The Prussian Army

Napoleon completely defeated the Prussian Army in 1806, and it was from 1808 onwards that the reformers under Scharnhorst and Gneisenau began to create a new force which was eventually to turn the tide of battle decisively against Napoleon at Waterloo.

The Prussian infantry consisted of line regiments, each of three battalions – two musketeer and one fusilier – and two companies of grenadiers. Each battalion consisted of four companies; the grenadiers were grouped into provincial battalions. The average strength of a battalion was some six or seven hundred men. Brigades consisted of three regiments, one regular, one reserve, and one *Landwehr* (recruited from a *levée en masse*). There were no divisions in the Prussian Army, but three or four brigades, together with artillery and one or two brigades of cavalry, constituted an army corps.

The Prussian Army included three, later four, rifle battalions and individual companies were allotted to different commands. These and the fusilier battalions provided the Army's skirmishing lines. In 1813, numerous volunteer *Jägers* joined the army, and in many cases they were equipped as riflemen and attached to the regular regiments.

Cavalry regiments fielded only two or three squadrons and were grouped into brigades, each with a strength of from seven to twelve squadrons. There was no reserve cavalry, but numerous regiments of *Landwehr* were raised and grouped in the brigades alongside regulars. The Prussian cavalry consisted of cuirassier, dragoon, hussar, and ulan regiments, the latter armed with a lance.

The Prussian artillery included foot batteries using 6- and 12-pounder cannon; the horse artillery also had 6-pounder pieces. Each battery consisted of six cannon and two howitzers.

Prior to 1806, Prussian tactics were essentially those of Frederick the Great, being based entirely upon the linear systems of the Seven Years' War. In 1812, a completely new doctrine modelled on the French pattern was adopted. However, the Prussians did not ape the French method of making mass attacks with enormous infantry columns. They used the column only as a means of manoeuvring and, since their army was relatively small before 1813, they managed to evolve a system of inter-arm cooperation. The infantry battalions formed columns, but they were aligned so that they could deploy at a moment's notice. The cavalry and artillery formed part of the regulation brigade advance and could thus be brought to the front if required. This mixed attack-force was mutually supporting, and it was not at all like the bludgeon employed by Napoleon's armies, despite the fact that it was based upon the close column.

Minor cavalry tactics were similar to those of the French, the attack being either in columns or in echelon, but, unlike the French, the massed cavalry attack was not utilized.

Prussian *Landwehr*, 1813

The Austrian Army

The Austrian line infantry were divided into Hungarian and German regiments; only their uniforms were different, the armament and organization being identical. Regiments seldom fielded more than two fusilier battalions, and each battalion contained three divisions of two companies. The established strength of a battalion was 840 men, but there were seldom more than four or five hundred men when in the field. In addition to its fusiliers, each regiment had a division of grenadiers, grouped into composite battalions and generally employed as the army reserve.

By 1813 the Army contained twelve *Jäger* battalions, light infantry units subdivided like the line infantry. The frontier troops, the Grenz Infantry, were also considered to be light infantry and they were always grouped with light cavalry in the advanced guard divisions of each army corps.

The Austrian cavalry was divided into heavy and light branches. The heavy cavalry regiments consisted of cuirassiers and dragoons, each with six squadrons and a full strength of about nine hundred men. The light cavalry – hussars, chevaulegers, and lancers – had eight squadrons with an establishment of a little over thirteen hundred men.

An infantry brigade usually consisted of two regiments with four or five battalions. Two brigades and two batteries formed a division, and three divisions an *Armee-Abteilung*. The first, or advanced, guard division of each *Armee-Abteilung* differed in that it was always a mixed force of light infantry and cavalry. The grenadiers and heavy cavalry, with some line divisions, formed the army reserve. Austrian tactics, like those of the other continental powers, were greatly influenced by the French system. The infantry were drilled in the use of a line, but usually manoeuvred in a column of divisions. The basic infantry formation was a three-deep line, of which one rank was theoretically intended to act as skirmishers, but an entrenched attitude amongst line officers meant that this was seldom the case. Skirmishers were usually provided from the light troops and in the *Jäger* battalion one third of the men were armed with rifles.

The artillery consisted of three different types of battery: generally static position batteries of four or six 12-pounder cannon, brigade batteries of eight 3- or 6-pounder pieces attached to the infantry brigades and worked mainly in direct support of the command to which they were subordinated, and cavalry batteries. The latter, of six 6-pounder cannon, formed a mobile reserve, but they were not true horse artillery as used by the other powers.

Cavalry tactics were based on small troop columns which formed alongside each other to present a deep line. Regiments attacked by divisions, each of two squadrons, and the regiment always held back part of its strength as a reserve.

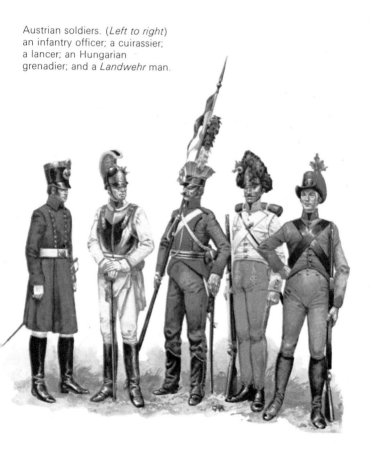

Austrian soldiers. (*Left to right*) an infantry officer; a cuirassier; a lancer; an Hungarian grenadier; and a *Landwehr* man.

The Russian Army

The army of the Czar had a rigid peace-time organization. The major unit was a division and this contained six infantry or cavalry regiments. Two regiments formed a brigade and two divisions generally comprised an army corps.

Infantry regiments were divided into three battalions, each of four companies, with a full battalion establishment of 738 men. Each company consisted of two platoons. Generally, after 1810, each battalion contained three centre companies, called 'fusiliers' or 'musketeers' in the grenadier and musketeer regiments respectively. The senior company in both types of regiment was designated 'grenadier', and its two platoons were placed to the left and the right of a battalion line. The men of one platoon were known as 'grenadiers' and those of the other as 'tuirailleurs'. The light infantry regiments were similarly organized, with the centre companies bearing the designation '*Jäger*', and after 1810 the élite company was referred to as '*Jäger*-grenadiers'.

The mounted branch of the Army consisted of cuirassiers, dragoons, hussars, ulans, and cossacks. The line cavalry regiments, as well as the hussars and ulans of the Guard, each contained five squadrons. The other Guard regiments consisted of ten squadrons, except for the Guard cossacks, which had only three. Line squadrons had an establishment of 151 men, whereas that of the Guard was slightly larger at 159. In addition to the regular cavalry, Russia possessed a large force of irregulars – the cossacks. These horsemen operated in swarms and were of incalculable value to the Russian Army.

The artillery was divided into foot, horse, and garrison units. The highest permanent artillery formation was the brigade, which consisted of three companies – two light and one heavy. The brigades were attached throughout the army at corps level. Each company had a strength of twelve pieces – eight cannon and four unicorns – the latter being large-calibre pieces capable of firing a shell but with a longer barrel than the conventional howitzer. Light companies contained 6-pounder cannon and 10-pounder unicorns, and the heavy companies had 12-pounder cannon and 20-pounder unicorns. Several brigades were always held back as an army reserve and these units contained the light horse-artillery companies.

Traditionally, the Russian Army consisted of an officer corps drawn from the nobility and ranks filled from the peasantry. This produced an army with several distinct characteristics. The Russian soldier seldom retreated in rout; if there was no officer to order a retirement, then he stood fast, where his last order had positioned him. His endurance was phenomenal and his obedience implicit, both natural extensions of serfdom.

The Russian Army used a tactical system based upon the heavy column and not dissimilar to that of the Prussian Army. Skirmishers were provided by the tuirailleur platoons of each infantry battalion and it is notable that one brigade of each division was generally composed entirely of light-infantry regiments. The Russians were the only power to adopt the rifle in large quantities and much of the light infantry was armed with this weapon.

Russian soldiers, 1812–14. (*Left to right*) a musketeer; a cuirassier; a cossack; and a horse artilleryman.

Westphalian infantry, c. 1812

The minor states

The numerous other large and small states of Europe all participated in the Napoleonic Wars. Spain and Portugal, for example, fought against the French in the Peninsular War from 1808 to 1814. The Portuguese Army was largely influenced by Britain, and she provided a well-trained and organized force to fight alongside Wellington's armies.

In Italy, the Italian Kingdom and Naples were completely dominated by Napoleon. Poland, too, was upheld by Napoleon's might. Indeed, all three states were created to serve France's political and military interests and consequently their armies reflected French organization and tactics and many French officers served in their ranks. In Poland, the Grand Duchy of Warsaw raised large armies to fight for the French and one of her princes became a marshal of France. Polish troops were even taken into the French Army as an élite guard cavalry regiment. Holland and Belgium were an integral part of France from 1810, but fought against Napoleon in 1815.

One result of the French domination of Europe was the formation of the Confederation of the Rhine, which incorporated most of the smaller West German states. All the Confederation states were required to supply military contingents – in some cases only of company strength – and these were grouped into composite regiments.

The German kingdoms of Saxony, Bavaria, and Württemberg retained their independence throughout the Napoleonic Wars, and until the Battle of Leipzig in 1813 they generally fought alongside the French, providing brigades and divisions directly controlled by their own officers.

(Left to right) a Saxon infantryman; an officer in the Polish Lancers; a Bavarian infantryman; a Württemburg infantryman; and a gunner from the Grand Duchy of Berg.

THE AMERICAN CIVIL WAR

The American Civil War lasted from 1861 to 1865. It was fought between the industrial north of the United States – the Union – and the rural south – the Confederacy – and therein lies the main factor for the eventual victory of the North. In 1861, both armies were enthusiastic and strong. By the end of the war, the resources of the South were exhausted, both in manpower and material, whereas the North had never been stronger, its superior manpower and industrial capacity having been harnessed to crush the South. This disparity in resources imparted distinct characteristics to the rival armies. The North tended to be well provisioned, armed, and clothed, but the

Soldiers of the Civil War. (*Left to right*) North: an infantryman; a sergeant, Volunteer Cavalry; a zouave, 11th Indiana Volunteers; a general officer; and an artillery officer. South: a general officer; an infantry officer; a sergeant of infantry, full dress; an infantryman, 1861; and an infantryman, 1864.

South was always short on war material of all descriptions.

The American Civil War was important in the development of warfare because it can be described as the first modern conflict. Railway systems played an important part in troop transportation, automatic weapons made their appearance on the battlefield, and, for the first time, large quantities of rifled small-arms and artillery were available to the contestants. The widespread use of telegraphic communications, with a rapid dissemination of information direct from the battle areas, revolutionized warfare. And lastly, the operations around Richmond in 1864 even foreshadowed trench warfare of the First World War.

Despite the advances in military science that were displayed during the war, the vast area covered by the conflict inevitably made cavalry an important part of the armies. By the end of the Civil War, the Union cavalry was a large, well-equipped, and well-trained body which could operate in mounted or dismounted action, taking the part of mobile infantry or pure horsemen with equal ease. The method of its

employment gave an example which became the cornerstone in the argument for the retention of the cavalryman for the next fifty years.

Firepower

The standard infantry weapon used by soldiers from both the North and South a muzzle-loading rifle. Many different patterns were used, especially by the Confederacy, who imported large numbers of European firearms, but the principal rifle in use with the Northern forces was the ·58 calibre Model 1861 rifle musket, commonly known as the Springfield. The Model 1861 and the slightly modified 1863 and 1864 patterns had effective ranges of 500–600 yards. At 200–300 yards, these rifles were infallible, and they could kill at up to even 1,000 yards. At this long range, however, the

American Civil War weapons: a Remington revolver (A); an officer's sword (B); a Springfield rifle musket (C); a Remington rifle musket (D); an Enfield rifle musket (E); a Starr army revolver (F); and a Colt revolver (G).

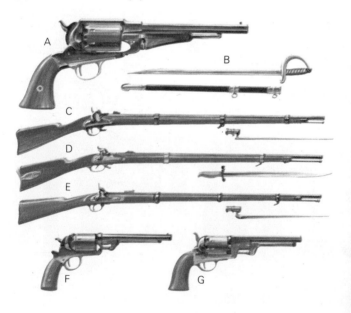

target had to be large, and even then a certain amount of good luck was also required. A well-trained soldier could fire three rounds per minute from the Springfield. Next to the Model 1861, the British ·577 Enfield was the most popular rifle, and both sides purchased it.

The Sharps breech-loading rifle was used essentially as a cavalry weapon. Some 80,000 were purchased by the Federal Government and they gave the Union horsemen a decided advantage over their adversaries. The real merit of the Sharps was that it could fire at some three times the rate of ordinary rifles. Pistols and revolvers were used in large numbers by cavalrymen, but these were close-combat weapons, being incapable of hitting a target at anything but a very short range.

Machine guns were available to both sides but were seldom used due to problems of mobility and ammunition supply.

The artillery used both smooth-bore and rifled pieces, breech- and muzzle-loaders, but the technical superiority of rifled guns was neutralized by difficulties in ammunition and fuse technology. Principal amongst the pieces of artillery used during the war was the 12-pounder gun-howitzer, Model 1857, the Napoleon. It had an effective range of 2,000 yards. The 6-pounder, which was the other equally common smooth bore, had a range that was only marginally less. Numerous types of rifled guns were employed, Whitworth's, Armstrong's and Parrott's amongst others. They had greater range and accuracy than the smooth bore, but they suffered from the major defect of having to fire a shell which buried itself in the ground before exploding.

Smooth-bore ammunition consisted of solid shot (which was used against buildings and masses of troops), shells (which were fired at earthworks as well), and a variety of case shot. Canister was used with deadly effect at ranges of up to 350 yards, and shrapnel at between 500 and 1,500 yards. Smooth-bore pieces could load and fire spherical case twice in a minute; solid shot had a similar rate of fire but with canister the piece could be loaded and discharged in roughly twenty seconds.

Siege and garrison artillery consisted of heavy pieces which could not be easily used in the field. Siege guns fired projectiles of up to 84 pounds, and the equally heavy fortress guns were on fixed mountings.

Tactics

The Union and Confederate Armies adopted similar tactical systems because the senior officers of both sides had been schooled in the United States Regular Army.

The infantry regiment consisted of ten companies and it fought in a two-deep battleline (see below). Attacks were launched by waves, one regiment or brigade behind another. The distance between waves varied from as little as 25 yards up to 300 yards. The intention was that a large gap be kept so that the second wave had room to manoeuvre to left or right and did not suffer from shots fired at the first wave. The infantry manuals quoted rates of march, in yards per minute: com-

A typical infantry battle formation of the Civil War. The main line consists of six companies; two companies are ranged in extended order as a skirmishing line and two are held in reserve.

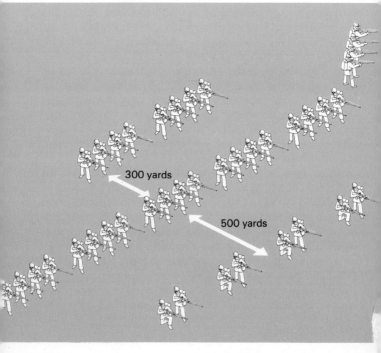

mon time, 70; quick time, 86; and double-quick time, 109.

Cavalry troops were manoeuvred in columns of four, and changes were executed in a double line, a single line being adopted by both sides after 1862. Marching cavalry could cover some four miles per hour; the manoeuvre trot doubled this speed, and the extended gallop doubled the speed again. For dismounted action, one man in four was told off as a horse holder.

All these details apply to the early stages of the war. The manuals available at the beginning of the war were formulated in a period when the only practical experience upon which to base manoeuvre and tactical regulations was combat with smooth-bore muskets. These near-Napoleonic concepts of battle proved completely unsuited to warfare with rifled weapons and so the tactical approach changed. The regimental skirmishing line, for instance, became half the regimental strength. The value of temporary fortifications was apparent to all, and so battlelines took cover – behind walls and any other protection that was available. If time permitted, breastworks were built and trenches dug. Greater emphasis began to be laid upon entrenching and the final battles in Virginia were very similar to certain phases of the Great War. Even mining and counter-mining operations were conducted.

Increased infantry firepower deprived the artillery of its traditional offensive role since gunners could not unlimber their pieces within canister range of an infantry formation. During the American Civil War, the artillery was definitely relegated to a supporting arm. Its main value in a battle was as a defensive weapon, utilizing canister shot against the attackers.

The field artillery provided the bulk of guns for the divisions and corps of the armies whereas the horse artillery was either attached to the cavalry or held in a central army reserve. The manoeuvre speeds of field and horse artillery were similar to those of cavalry. Batteries usually manoeuvred at the trot. Like the infantry, the gunners appreciated the value of cover and, if time allowed, earthworks were thrown up around their positions. In the field a battery of six guns had a theoretical front of 82 yards, 14 yards being allowed between pieces. Behind the battery the gun and the caisson teams were drawn up to a depth of 47 yards.

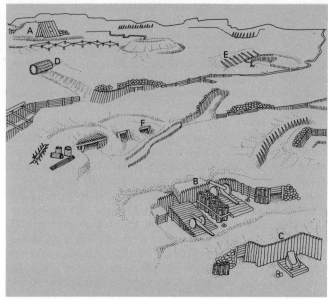

Typical American Civil War fortifications: a timber casement (A); artillery siege positions (B); a siege mortar or coehorn (C); a sap-roller, which could be moved forward to protect the men working behind it (D); sharpened stakes (E); and a dug-out (F).

The North

The Northern Armies were drawn from the twenty-three states that did not secede from the Union in 1861. They consisted of the pre-war United States Regular Army and the huge volunteer force which came into being upon the declaration of war.

The Regular Army was small, and in 1861 it was scattered over the country in numerous forts and frontier outposts, but much of it was later grouped into a complete division that served with the Army of the Potomac. When war broke out, many regular officers were faced with the decision of either leaving the Army and joining the South or staying and fighting for the Union. In effect, the pre-war regular officer corps provided the leadership of both armies, and opposing commanders had often served with one another or had been together at the military academy of West Point.

The volunteers were based on the old state militia, which constituted the senior regiments of the enlarged force. Each state was responsible for the recruitment of troops within its own area. The regiments were designated by a number and the name of the state of origin – for instance, 15th New York. The ten companies were lettered A to J. 'A' Company held the right of the line and was commanded by the senior captain. The full strength of an infantry regiment was a little over one thousand men and officers, but it was the Northern practice to create new units rather than maintain a regiment's strength. When a regiment fell to 150 or 200 men, it was broken up and distributed amongst others. The average Union infantry regiment in the spring of 1863 numbered 425 men.

At first, cavalry regiments consisted of twelve troops, each numbering 100 men, grouped into six squadons. In 1863, the strength of a troop was made variable, from eighty-two to one hundred men, and the squadron organization was dropped. At the same time, the cavalry battalion was introduced. This was intended for men on detached service and usually contained four troops.

Four regiments usually formed a brigade, although this number was subject to fluctuation. Three brigades formed a division. Two or three divisions were usually grouped together in a corps, but a corps could include up to five divisions.

Pieces of artillery were grouped into batteries, normally of six guns, but four-gun batteries were also common. In 1861, 12-pounder batteries usually contained four 12-pounder guns and two 24-pounder howitzers; 6-pounder batteries had four 6-pounder guns and two 12-pounder howitzers. Later in the war, there was a tendency to equip a battery with six similar pieces, the Union Army usually using 3-inch rifles, 10- or 20-pounder Parrotts, or 12-pounder Napoleons. Within the battery two guns formed a section, and one gun, together with its six-horse team, limber and crew, constituted a platoon, commanded by a sergeant. Four batteries were attached to each division and usually half of the divisional artillery was withdrawn to form a corps reserve. Additionally, each army had its reserve of heavy and horse batteries.

A Confederate charge

Until 1863, engineering functions were performed by men detailed from infantry regiments under the direction of engineer officers. In that year, two engineer regiments of skilled artisans were organized on infantry-regiment lines.

A signal corps was organized in August 1864. Prior to that date, the signal troops had operated in a disjointed fashion because of inter-departmental rivalry in Washington. Despite this rivalry, the importance of quick communication was early realized by the government, and it is significant that by an Act of Congress in 1862 all the private telegraph lines and offices in the country were taken over by the Army.

The South

As already mentioned, the Confederate Armies, unlike their Northern counterparts, tended to be increasingly ill equipped and clothed as the end of the war drew closer. Frequently they would obtain supplies of war material and clothing from the

debris of the battlefield, their weapons and accoutrements often bearing the stampings of a Federal arsenal, but even this source of supply diminished as the South won fewer victories. The Confederacy had only a small industrial capacity and was forced to augment its inadequate supply of weapons by large-scale purchases from Europe. The consequence of obtaining such a variety of weapons was a lack of uniformity in the equipment of the front-line troops.

Southern infantry regiments were organized on a basis similar to those of the North. The fundamental difference between them was that the South provided, to the best of its ability, a flow of recruits to the existing units. Thus the original regiments were sustained throughout the war and their spirit was preserved despite the fact that they were frequently reduced to mere skeletons. As originally in the North, the Southern regiments were based on the state militia that had existed prior to 1861.

One of the South's few advantages was the existence of its landed gentry and farmers, whose lives centred upon the horse. These two social classes provided the Confederate Armies with a reservoir of natural horsemen who were formed into superb mounted units. Cavalry regiments consisted of ten squadrons, each with a strength of between sixty and eighty men. Two to six regiments were grouped into a brigade, and up to six brigades formed a division. The decline of the Southern cavalry towards the end of the war can be mainly attributed to a shortage of horses.

Infantry brigades were formed by grouping together several regiments, usually from the same state. The number varied but four was normal. The higher structure of the Southern Army was similar to that of the North. However, there were far fewer major units and divisions, and brigades were known by the name of the commander, Hood's Texans, for instance. Very often the name of a formation's original commander was retained for a considerable time after the command had changed hands.

A typical dismounted cavalry battleline. Behind the main line are the horse holders and a skirmishing line is in advance.

The artillery was formed into battalions, each of four batteries and each battery having four guns. It was considered quite a normal occurrence for the four guns in a battery to be of three different types and calibres. This was the inevitable result of material shortages and made the problem of ammunition supply even more complicated than usual. Normally one battalion was attached to each division and several more were given to each corps to act as its reserve. In the initial stages of the war, large numbers of 6-pounders were in use, but these were mainly replaced by 12-pounder Napoleons and 3-inch rifled guns. Lee is on record as recommending that, if insufficient metal was available for new guns, the 6- and 12-pounder howitzers should be smelted to provide metal for 12-pounder Napoleons.

The supporting branches of the Confederate Army tended to be only shadows of their Northern counterparts. The medical system was efficient and well developed, but the other branches were entirely insufficient to meet the demands imposed upon them by the war.

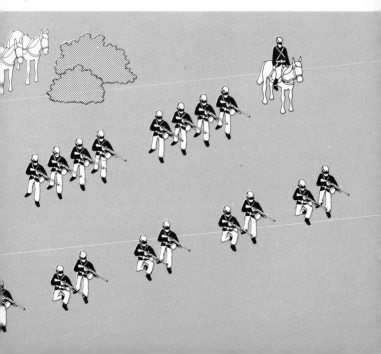

British paratrooper, 1944. Airborne operations are an element of warfare peculiar to the post-1939 period.

THE SECOND WORLD WAR

The war of 1939–45 was fought between the Axis Powers – Germany, Japan, and Italy – and the Allies, Great Britain, the United States, Russia, and China. Many other countries were involved at one stage or another, but the main protagonists were those noted above.

Operations were conducted in several completely different theatres, the North African desert, the steppes of Russia, and the jungles of Burma, to name but three. The navies battled both on and beneath the seas, and vast air forces fought in the skies above. This was a war of truly global dimensions.

It is also a war which offers the wargamer an infinite variety of situations and problems. Terrain must be realistic and must also take account of the season. The frozen winters of the Eastern Front or the sands of the desert can both be represented, along with other settings that may be required. Climatic extremes will affect the rules of a game, but this fact and the matter of terrain are mere details when compared with weapon technology, the one important aspect of the Second World War which sets it apart from our other two periods.

Weapon technology produced an almost infinite variety of armaments, and the availability of new weapons necessitated new techniques for handling them. The most important single weapon was the armoured fighting vehicle – the tank – and all Western armies were to base their tactics upon its use. It was essentially a vehicle of offence and thus anti-tank weapons were developed to provide the keystone of defence. To give support to tanks and, increasingly, to counter the growing numbers of anti-tank weapons, large forces of mechanized infantry and artillery accompanied the armoured vehicles in their forward thrusts. Attempts to counter the masses of tanks that were committed in the second half of the war resulted in a wide variety of anti-tank devices, such as mines, guns, and rockets. These grew more effective as time went on, but they in turn led to more powerful tanks.

Linked to the concept of mobile armoured warfare was the use of air power. Aircraft could operate far behind the enemy front, disrupting supply lines and breaking communications. Airborne troops could be landed to seize key points such as bridges, and domination of the sky above a battlefield became almost a prerequisite for ground victory.

The tank dominated the war in Europe and Africa. In the East, however, the terrain was not generally suited to mechanized warfare, and the armies that fought in Burma and the Pacific relied more on the soldierly virtues of their men than on materials.

The seaborne attacks across the Pacific produced tactics of their own which, when coupled with the character of the Japanese, resulted in a style of warfare completely unlike that which was being waged in Europe. Resourcefulness, guile, and endurance counted for more than material superiority. The role of air power was also different, its primary use being to support the large fleets that operated in the vast areas of sea amidst which were scattered the contested islands.

The German Tiger tank

Armour

As has already been stated, armour and the effect that it had upon military thinking were of paramount importance in shaping the tactics of the Second World War.

The aggressive use of the tank was first demonstrated by the Germans. Their concept of armoured warfare, *Blitzkrieg*, called for a massed tank attack on a defensive zone. Once the desired penetration had been achieved, the armour was intended to sweep on into the interior of the country and eventually cause a complete breakdown in the enemy's will and ability to continue the fight. Centres of resistance were by-passed since tanks had to avoid becoming bogged down in combat. The whole basis of *Blitzkrieg* was speed. Behind the tanks came the slow-moving infantry which 'mopped up' such opposition as had not been eliminated by the initial armoured advance. The Germans did not imagine that this could be accomplished by tanks alone. Water crossings were to be seized by airborne troops and the Luftwaffe was conceived largely as a supporting force of flying artillery, to be used in conjunction with the armoured spearheads.

The Germans also integrated their tanks into mixed forces,

90

the Panzer divisions. Within these divisions were all the components of a small army. The tanks could be supported by infantry or vice versa; both could be assisted by artillery; reconnaissance, engineer, and communication elements were also included. The main characteristic of the Panzer divisions was that they were completely motorized and were thus capable of rapid movement. The greatest German victories were all won against armies that did not include equivalents to the Panzer divisions, and all the combatant nations in Europe eventually provided their armies with similar organizations, thus depriving the Germans of their monopoly in this sphere.

In the later years of the war, attempts at a breakthrough usually developed into full-scale tank battles. However, unless the attackers possessed an overwhelming superiority of armour, they would fail because of an abundance of effective anti-tank weapons. These had been absent at the time of the great German triumphs.

The armoured vehicle which caused this dramatic change in the mode of warfare was first used during the First World War. Successful development between the wars produced

The *'Wespe'*, a German self-propelled gun

vast numbers of tanks by 1939, but, except for those of the German Army, they tended to be ineffective since they were envisaged as auxiliaries to the infantry. The mobile role of armour was later accepted by all countries, but the tanks that were developed during the war tended to be more heavily armoured as each new design endeavoured to overcome the increasing effectiveness of anti-tank artillery.

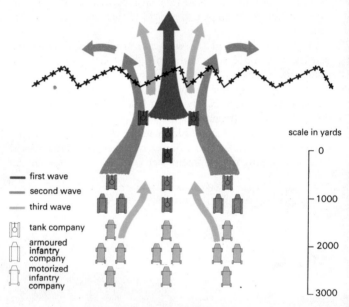

scale in yards

first wave
second wave
third wave

tank company
armoured infantry company
motorized infantry company

German armoured assault tactics. Wave 1 penetrated the enemy's defences. Wave 2 widened the gap, ready for the advance of Wave 3.

Much has been written on the technical aspects of tanks, but one point is, none the less, worth making. Apart from mechanical reliability, the combat value of any tank rests upon its armament. The standard design fault in most Second World War tanks was that their main gun was added almost as an afterthought. With few exceptions, the first generation of tanks were undergunned. The 2-pounder gun fitted to

British tanks was ineffective against anything but the lightest of armour. The armament of the German Panzers I, II, and III was little better, the Panzer I being armed only with machine guns. Early Russian and American tanks were similarly equipped. The German Panzer IV carried a 75mm gun and this set the pattern for later development, guns of a similar calibre being fitted in the British Churchills, American Shermans, and the Russian T34s, all of which were in wide use during the later part of the war. The decision by the Western Allies to mount heavier guns sprang from the experiences of 1940–1, but by the time they were in service the German Panzer IV had been made obsolete by the Panther and Tiger. The latter was constructed along normal German design principles but mounted an 88mm gun, whereas the Panther, although armed with a long 75mm piece, had sloping armour based on that of the Russian T34. The T34's sloping armour was very effective in the deflection of shells and had first been met by the Germans with considerable bewilderment in 1941; thus the Panther demonstrated the Germans' ability to learn from others. The last German battle tank was the so-called 'King Tiger', which combined the design characteristics of the Panther with the 88mm gun. It appeared on the battlefields in 1944 and prompted the Allies to new and heavier designs which were being committed to combat for the first time when the war ended.

Firepower

Firepower during the Second World War is the most difficult of factors to assess because of the vast number of weapon types used by the combatant nations. In wars prior to the twentieth century, armies were equipped with weapons which, although of different pattern and manufacture, tended to be fairly similar in performance. Whereas this generalization can be applied to certain categories of weapons used between 1939 and 1945, there are distinct inequalities in others. For example, the performances of the German 98 and the American Springfield, both standard infantry bolt-action rifles, were strikingly similar: both having 5-round magazines and effective ranges of 600–800 yards, with maximum ranges of about 2,500 yards. In terms of wargaming, the

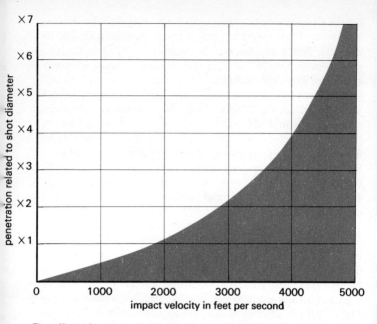

The effect of armour-piercing shot on armoured plate: a proof of the formula described on page 96. The 8·8cm Pak. 43, with a muzzle velocity of 3,594fps at 250 yards, has a penetration of roughly three times the shot diameter (3×88mm = 264mm).

differences that existed between these rifles are of almost no significance. When one examines heavy anti-tank guns, however, the German 8·8 Pak. had no equal. The '88' was a phenomenal gun which combined a rapidity of fire with a high degree of accuracy; its armour-piercing projectile was capable of penetrating the thickest of Allied armour. The value of this weapon is emphasized by the fact that, although Allied anti-tank gun development was beginning to rival that of Germany at the end of the war, the Germans had been using their '88', in one form or another, since 1939.

Another significant point when assessing firepower is time: data should always relate to the same time period. Performance figures for a Vicker's machine gun differed little between 1939 and 1945, but the German 75mm gun fitted into tanks underwent a considerable evolution during the war.

The 75's barrel was lengthened to give a much greater muzzle velocity, and the resulting weapon was the standard armament on the Panzer IVs and Panthers at the end of the war. Thus, before attempting to formulate rules covering their use, it is important to know not only the weapons' characteristics but also how long the various armies used them.

The fire effect of heavier weapons depended mainly on fire-control equipment. The science of artillery was, and is, very exact. Direct fire called for the use of sophisticated range finders. The excellence of this equipment and the ability of its users to interpret their readings correctly could be the difference between life and death, especially in tank combat. British and American fire-control equipment was adequate, but that of the Germans was superb. It has been suggested that the main reason why the Germans were not completely overwhelmed by the masses of Russian tanks encountered on the Eastern Front was that they had excellent optical equipment – sights, range finders, etc. – and the Russians had no such aids or only very crude ones. Indirect fire was aimed at a map reference and was called down by an observer who could see the target and the shell bursts. He then gave a correction which was converted into degrees of traverse or elevation at the gun position. Once the correct range and bearing had been established, rapid fire followed. If artillery was in one position for any length of time, certain possible targets were registered and recorded so that an instantaneous barrage could be laid if required. As soon as the guns were moved, these recorded ranges were rendered useless.

The most complicated aspect of fire effect in the modern period is undoubtedly that of anti-tank gunnery: there are so many factors which have to be taken into account. Firstly, the gun itself dictates its armour-piercing capability by the weight of its shot and its muzzle velocity. Then, the tank must be seen as a target with different thicknesses of armour covering its different parts; the front and sides usually had thicker armour than the top, and the rear was the least protected part of the vehicle.

The penetration of a shot is determined by its weight and its velocity at the moment of impact. A completely accurate figure for velocity can be obtained only by consulting the

The German '88' with its anti-tank/anti-aircraft mounting

ballistics tables for each piece of artillery concerned, but, since this is not always possible, the simple equation noted here offers a fairly accurate method for determining this important point. The formula used is $F = \dfrac{250}{C}$. F is the percentage loss in velocity over the 250 yards from a known velocity. C is the calibre in millimetres. For example, the 88mm Pak. 43, firing armour-piercing ammunition, had a muzzle velocity of 3,705 feet per second. Now $\dfrac{250}{88}$ equals an approximate loss of velocity of three per cent. Three per cent of 3,705 is 111; take this from the muzzle velocity and a figure of 3,594 is obtained. This is the velocity of an armour-piercing shell at 250 yards from the muzzle of the gun. For every successive 250 yards, the previous velocity is reduced by three per cent. (See the graph on page 94.)

Tactics

Although tactics differed between the combatant armies, there are, none the less, certain generalizations that can be made.

Defensive tactics were based on 'fields of fire', these being areas which could be effectively covered by particular weapons. Weapons were, therefore, sited where they could do the maximum damage to an attacker and, since weapon sites ideally afforded concealment and protection to the weapon users, they became fortifications – to a lesser or greater extent depending upon the available time.

In mobile warfare, weapons were positioned as opportunity allowed – in ditches, houses, behind hedges, and so on – but, if given even a few hours, a seemingly innocent countryside could be transformed into a strong defensive area. The primary instrument in this transformation was the entrenching tool which all infantrymen carried; in normal conditions a shallow rifle pit, or 'fox hole', could be excavated in minutes. Obstacles which limited fields of fire – such as small bushes – were removed, and, if possible, similar features which could afford concealment to an advancing enemy were also cleared. Temporary positions were always situated at the most advantageous points – on hilltops and in farm houses – or integrated into already existing natural obstacles, such as the thick hedgerows found in Normandy. If sufficient time was available, strong points were linked by networks of trenches, the simple rifle pits became dug-outs, capable of withstanding artillery fire, and the whole defensive area was protected by belts of barbed wire and minefields, which were intended to force the attackers to conform to the defenders' plans. Really strong and more permanent defensive positions, such as the Atlantic Wall *circa* 1944, utilized concrete emplacements and numerous other refined obstacles in addition to those mentioned already.

In the Pacific and Burma, the nature of the terrain made certain tactical variations inevitable. Dense jungle reduced the effective range of weapons, and concealment consequently

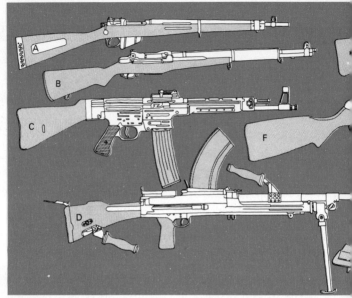

Weapons of the Second World War: the British Lee Enfield rifle, No. 4, Mk I (A); the American Garand (B); the German MP 43 (C); the British Bren gun (D); the American Browning automatic rifle (E); the Russian PPSH 1941 (F); and the Japanese Nambu machine gun (G).

gained greater importance. On Pacific coral islands, it was impossible to dig more than a few feet without becoming waterlogged, therefore fortifications were erected rather than excavated.

No single line of defensive positions was capable of stopping a determined attack by armoured forces and so armies resorted to the German First World War concept of defence in depth. Systems of mutually supporting positions, interlaced with barbed-wire entanglements and minefields, were built up to a depth of several miles, and their strength was sufficient to blunt any assault. It was possible to create additional depth to a system even whilst battle was in progress. Russian tactics during the Battle of Kursk in 1943 were an outstanding example of this type of defence.

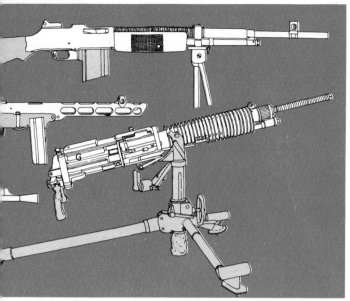

Although the attackers always held an advantage, since it was they who selected the point of battle, assaults could be costly operations. This was especially so towards the end of the war when anti-tank gun efficiency began to lessen the value of armour. It is worth remembering that a tank could be completely destroyed by a variety of anti-tank devices, none of which cost anything like as much as the tank. If the armoured assault broke through the defensive zone and then drove into the enemy's interior, the cost was well rewarded, but the attackers frequently suffered very heavy losses only to be confronted by the defenders' untouched tank force in the area immediately behind the defensive zone.

Offensive tactics were designed to break through barriers such as those described earlier, and their success largely depended upon the nature of the defences. The German *Blitzkrieg* theory has already been mentioned (see page 90), and its efficiency relied upon cooperation within the service. The tanks formed the spearhead of the division, but, if an obstacle more suited to assault by infantry was encountered,

Radio plays an important part in modern wargaming.

such as a series of anti-tank gun emplacements, then the advance was taken over by the Panzer-grenadiers.

The attacker's one great advantage was that his artillery could be concentrated in secret before an assault and could thus provide overwhelming support at the correct point. Attacks were generally preceded by a barrage that was short in duration but intense in effort, being designed to cause the maximum damage to the defenders and to give the minimum warning of an impending assault.

Minor offensive tactics varied in detail between the armies, but essentially they consisted of units being split into those that were actually advancing and those that gave fire support, the two groups leapfrogging one over the other. The subject of minor tactics is extensive and complicated, and it is possible to evolve entire wargames based on the regulated minor tactical systems of the different armies.

Communications

Communications have always been an important aspect of warfare, but the Second World War was the first conflict in which radio was used on a large scale and it is questionable whether the war could have evolved as it did without radio. The fast-moving armoured columns could keep in touch with each other only by radio, and its widespread use made possible instant artillery support to any part of a battlefield that was within range of the guns. Radio also intensified the old problem of security of communication – plans could be uncovered by monitoring enemy radio signals. A wide use of codes was the inevitable result.

Infantry radio sets were generally capable of both reception and transmission, and had ranges of up to ten miles. Sets carried in armoured fighting vehicles were less efficient, with ranges in some instances of only two miles, but they were, none the less, fully adequate for their intended task, communication between individual tanks. Larger sets with much greater ranges were installed in command vehicles and these provided contact between units and higher commands and also fulfilled other functions, such as relaying messages for air support.

The basis of radio communication control was a network, the 'net' as it was known in the British service. Each net consisted of a number of sets all tuned to one frequency and therefore all in unbroken contact. Each unit had its own net and each commander was thus fully informed about, and capable of giving orders to, those under his control. In general, American, British, and German armies were well equipped with radio sets, the Russian armies were ill provided by Western standards, and the Japanese, although they had radios, placed great reliance upon wire communications.

Telephone systems were extensively used by all armies, but, excepting the Japanese, their function was mainly restricted to areas well behind the battlelines and to static defensive positions. Their major disadvantage was that their wires were easily cut by artillery fire.

The British 25-pounder field gun-howitzer

The British Army

In 1939, Britain was ill prepared for war, but, as usual in time
of national emergency, she rose to the challenge, and by 1945
her forces were amongst the finest in the world, amply armed
with weapons which, in many cases, had been developed
during the conflict.

Infantry divisions varied in composition. One type consisted of three brigades, two of infantry and one of tanks; six
regiments of artillery, three field, one medium, one anti-tank,
and one light anti-aircraft; a divisional reconnaissance regiment, and supporting services. More common, however, was
a division which included three infantry brigades and no
armoured element. All brigades contained three infantry
battalions and the battalion was the basic tactical unit. Each
consisted of a headquarters and four rifle companies. With
the headquarters were mortar, signals, pioneer, and anti-
aircraft platoons, as well as a carrier platoon that had thirteen
Bren-gun carriers on its strength. The rifle companies were
each composed of three platoons and a headquarters. Each
platoon was subdivided into three sections and these were
formed from ten men who were armed with one Bren gun,

seven rifles, and one sub-machine gun. Motorized infantry battalions, which formed the infantry brigades in the armoured divisions, were of an identical structure but were entirely motorized. The motor battalions – the infantry attached to the independent armoured brigades – differed from motorized battalions in that each company had three motor platoons and a scout platoon mounted in carriers. Their more powerful armament made them the strongest of British infantry formations.

Artillery regiments contained three batteries, each of two troops. The troops were subdivided into sections, each with two guns. Field artillery regiments were armed with 25-pounder gun-howitzers, a similar armament to that used by the completely mechanized Royal Horse Artillery regiments attached to the armoured divisions. Medium artillery used both the 4·5-inch gun and the 5·5-inch gun-howitzer.

Armoured divisions were formed from one armoured brigade, one motorized infantry brigade, and an armoured car regiment, as well as supporting artillery, engineers, signals, etc. The armoured brigade had a headquarters with ten tanks, three tank regiments, and an infantry motor battalion. The tank regiment's headquarters contained four tanks and ten armoured scout cars. Its three squadrons each had five troops of three tanks with an additional four tanks forming the headquarters. Armoured brigades had a full establishment of 193 tanks. Independent army tank brigades had a total of 78 tanks.

The following weapons were widely used by the British Army:

Lee Enfield No 1, Mk 3, ·303 calibre rifle Effective range: 600 yards. Maximum range: 2,000 yards. 10-round magazine. Rate of fire per minute: 5 rounds normal; 15 rounds rapid.
Bren light machine gun Effective range: 600–800 yards when mounted on a bipod. Maximum range: 2,000 yards. 30-round magazine.
Vickers medium machine gun Effective range: 400 yards. Maximum range: 2,000 yards. Belt fed.
6-pounder anti-tank gun (57mm) Muzzle velocity: 2,700 feet per second. Weight of shot: 6·25 pounds.
25-pounder field gun-howitzer Maximum range: 13,400 yards,

British soldiers, 1939–45. (*Left to right*) an officer, North Africa, 1941; a private, Burma, 1943; a private, Northern Europe, 1944; and a corporal, North Africa, 1942.

when using supercharge. Muzzle velocity: 1,747 feet per second. Weight of armour-piercing shot: 20 pounds.

Although the British Army was committed to a policy of offence, it is interesting to note that it recognized the value of defence. At the beginning of the war, a system of defence in depth was favoured, but experience in France and the Western Desert taught that it was better to concentrate force into small, well-armed pockets of resistance. Platoons took position so as to support their neighbours, and in this way a company defensive system was built up. The same logic was applied at company and battalion level.

The United States Army

Of all the armies that fought during the Second World War, the United States Army was the most lavishly equipped. It was dominated by the theory that firepower was the most important element in battle, and in the vast quantity of its equipment and the benefits that this conferred, it could not be faulted.

Armoured divisions contained two armoured regiments with a total of two light and four medium tank battalions, having a strength of 390 tanks. Supporting the armour was an armoured infantry regiment, an artillery regiment, and engineer, reconnaissance, ordnance, signals, and medical elements. In 1943 this pattern of organization was changed and a new type of armoured division – known as 'light', as opposed to 'heavy' – was introduced. The tank force was concentrated into three battalions, each with four companies instead of the previous three and with a total strength of 263 tanks. Both types of armoured division were used during the rest of the war.

Infantry divisions contained three regiments, which in turn were each divided into three battalions. The basic unit

American soldiers, 1944. (*Left to right*) a paratrooper; an infantryman; an infantryman in tropical combat dress; an officer in combat dress; and an infantryman in jungle camouflage.

The American M7 Priest, a self-propelled gun

upon which the higher infantry structure was built was the rifle squad and this consisted of twelve men, one of whom carried an automatic rifle (BAR). Rifle squads were grouped into threes to form platoons and these were similarly joined to form companies. Three companies made a battalion of twenty-seven rifle squads. Mortar and machine-gun squads were distributed at platoon and company level, and each battalion had a headquarters company. The regiment included specific infantry-gun and anti-tank companies.

Taken as a whole, the infantry regiment was armed with a galaxy of weapons ranging from rifles and carbines to towed howitzers. The principles governing equipment distribution were that at platoon level all weapons were completely portable; in the company, all weapons were portable to the extent that, if necessary, they could be manhandled with relative ease for between 80 and 100 yards; and all heavier equipment was attached at battalion and regimental level. The wide use of numerous automatic and specialist weapons designed to impart heavy firepower meant that in a regiment less than a third of its total strength carried rifles.

The following weapons were used by the United States Army:

·30 M1 Gerand semi-automatic rifle Sighted to 1,200 yards. 8-round magazine.

·30 M1 carbine Effective range: 300 yards. Maximum range: 2,000 yards. 15-round box magazine.

·30 Browning automatic rifle (BAR) Effective range: 600 yards. 20-round box magazine. Fired either semi or fully automatically.

·50 machine gun Maximum range: 7,200 yards. Belt fed.

60mm M19 mortar Range: 200 to 1,985 yards. Rate of fire: 30–35 bombs per minute.

57mm M1 anti-tank gun Maximum range: 10,000 yards. Muzzle velocity: 2,700 feet per second. Weight of shot: 6·28 pounds.

75mm field gun Maximum range: 13,600 yards.

105mm howitzer Maximum range: 12,200 yards.

An American 105mm howitzer in action

The Russian Army

The main military advantage that has always been enjoyed by Russia is that of quantity. Her population has always been capable of sustaining a very large army, and during the Second World War her industry, with American and British help, proved capable of arming her enormous land forces. The Red Army was ill equipped by Western standards, but such deficiencies as existed did not affect its basic fighting strength. The fact that many of its weapons were unsophisticated, that its tanks were often unfinished, with neither radios nor adequate fire-control equipment, and that the comforts of life were non-existent, did not worry the Russians. Consistently, after 1943, there was an abundance of men, tanks, weapons, and ammunition at the required points. What the Red Army lacked in quality, it made up for in quantity.

Russian armour was divided into three types: units that were intended for infantry support, independent tank regiments and brigades, and pure armoured formations – the tank corps – which were roughly equivalent to Western armoured

Russian soldiers, 1941–5. (*Left to right*) an infantryman; an infantryman in winter dress; 3rd and 5th figures, infantrymen in campaign dress; and an artillery officer.

divisions. Each of the latter had three tank brigades and a motorized infantry regiment. The tank brigades had three battalions, each of two squadrons, and a sub-machine gun battalion which, although armed with mortars and anti-tank weapons, had most of its personnel equipped as pure shock troops who rode into battle on the tanks. The tank squadrons consisted of two platoons, each with three troops of three tanks. Corps artillery was provided by two self-propelled regiments (one with twenty 85mm guns and the other with twenty 122mm howitzers), an anti-tank regiment, a heavy mortar regiment, and a rocket-launcher unit armed with the multi-barrelled Katyusha.

The motorized infantry divisions – the mechanized corps – were of a similar structure to the tank corps, but their basic elements were one tank brigade and three motorized infantry regiments.

The infantry, or rifle divisions, were weak by Western standards, averaging only some nine thousand men. Each consisted of three rifle regiments, an artillery regiment, and anti-tank, signals, and engineer battalions. The rifle regiments consisted of three battalions with two supporting anti-tank companies, as well as reconnaissance, artillery, and mortar companies. Each battalion had machine-gun and mortar companies, an anti-tank troop with two 57mm guns, and an anti-tank platoon with nine 45mm rifles; its main rifle contingent was formed into three companies. Each had three infantry platoons, a mortar platoon, and a machine-gun section. Platoons were based on four 9-man sections, whose main armament was the Degtyarew light machine gun. The artillery regiments had three battalions with a total armament of twenty-four 76mm guns and twelve 122mm howitzers, an anti-tank battalion with twelve 57mm anti-tank guns, and an anti-aircraft company.

A considerable proportion of the Red Army's guns were grouped into complete artillery divisions that were used in the sectors where their employment was advantageous, and this compensated for the relative weakness of divisional artillery.

Details of the principal Russian weapons follow:
7·62mm Model 1891/30 rifle The basic infantry rifle. Sighted

Russian self-propelled guns: the SU 76 (*top*) and SU 152 (*bottom*).

to 2,000 metres (2,187 yards). Effective range: 500 yards. 5-round magazine. Rate of fire: 10 rounds per minute.

PPSH 1941 sub-machine gun Sighted to 500 metres (547 yards). Effective range: 200 yards. Fed by a drum magazine with a 71-round capacity or a box holding 35 rounds.

DT 1929 machine gun (Degtyarew) Sighted to 1,500 metres (1,640 yards). Effective range: 800 yards. Fed by a drum magazine holding 47 rounds.

50mm Model 1940 mortar Range: 100–800 yards. Rate of fire: 30 bombs per minute.

57mm anti-tank gun Maximum range: 7,700 yards. Muzzle velocity: 2,140 feet per second. Weight of shot: 8·19 pounds.

76mm Model 1942 field gun Maximum range: 12,200 yards.

122mm Model 1938 howitzer Maximum range: 12,800 yards.

The Russian Army of 1941 was a force that was deficient in equipment, leadership, and general military knowledge. By

1943, it had served its apprenticeship in modern warfare, and its command, supply structure, and general ability were equal to any demand that was made upon it. The Russian offensive tactics of 1943–5 were essentially those of any army which possessed an overwhelming strength. Massive attacks were launched, and heavy casualties were of little significance as long as the objectives were accomplished.

The German Army

The German Army consisted of troops who were usually well trained, led, and equipped. The state of the army which conquered most of Europe was excellent, but, after the major defeat of Stalingrad (Winter 1942–3) and the capitulation of her forces in North Africa (May 1943), Germany found it increasingly difficult to maintain supplies of equipment and recruits to the front-line armies and the quality of her forces consequently began to decline. After 1943, the German Army

German soldiers. (*Left to right*) an SS gunner in the armoured artillery, 1943; an SS artillery NCO in winter dress, 1944; an Africa corps officer, 1941; and an infantryman, 1939.

The six-barrelled German rocket-launcher *'Nebelwerfer'*

tended to be under strength and under equipped and its soldiers were not of the same excellence as before. The Army suffered additionally from the formation of the Waffen SS, which underwent considerable expansion, always claiming the best of equipment and men.

The main strength of the German Army lay in its Panzer divisions. In 1944, these consisted of one Panzer regiment and two Panzer-grenadier regiments (one armoured and the other motorized), plus supporting troops including an anti-tank battalion. Each Panzer regiment contained two battalions, one of Panthers and the other of Mark IVs. Each battalion consisted of a headquarters, a support company which included fuel, munitions, maintenance, and administration sections, and three Panzer companies. A company had three platoons, each with four tanks. The Panzer-grenadiers were completely mobile and each regiment contained engineer and headquarter companies, a self-propelled gun company, and two battalions of Panzer-grenadiers, either motorized or armoured. Each battalion had headquarters, support, and heavy-weapon companies, in addition to its basic strength of three Panzer-grenadier companies, each of four platoons, including a machine-gun unit. The platoons contained a full establishment of forty-two men and NCOs, armed with twenty-six rifles, thirteen pistols, four sub-machine guns and six light machine guns; the whole unit was carried in five vehicles, armoured half-tracks in the armoured battalions.

The Panzer-grenadier divisions, which supported the main armoured units, were not dissimilar in organization to the Panzer divisions, the main difference being that neither Panzer-grenadier regiment was armoured and they included only one Panzer battalion instead of a regiment.

Several types of infantry division existed. The standard type contained three infantry regiments, each of three battalions with additional anti-tank and howitzer companies, an artillery regiment of four battalions, and the appropriate supporting units. The 1944-pattern division had infantry regiments with only two battalions. A few divisions were also formed with only two infantry regiments but each had three full battalions. Infantry battalions contained a headquarters, a heavy-weapon company, and three rifle companies. The rifle companies had three platoons and a heavy machine-gun section. Rifle platoons held thirty-three men, divided between three squads and a headquarters, and armed with twenty-two rifles, five pistols, seven sub-machine guns, and four light machine guns.

Apart from the merely administrative units which each division contained, every type had a number of combat units that played a supporting role to the main elements already noted. Principal amongst them were the artillery regiments. Guns were grouped into battalions, generally of three batteries. In armoured formations some of the guns were self-propelled. In the infantry divisions a great reliance was placed on the horse as a means of pulling equipment. The engineer battalions were combat pioneers who were quite capable of playing an active part in the fighting. The pioneer units in armoured formations were fully mechanized, even armoured, and they often formed the front wave of an attack since it was they who carried special equipment such as flame throwers and mine detectors. Anti-tank battalions were again self-propelled in the Panzer and Panzer-grenadier divisions or on a more modest scale for the rest of the army. The signals battalion provided a coordinating network for controlling an entire division and was armed with nothing heavier than light machine guns. And finally, each division contained a reconnaissance battalion, whose composition varied considerably. In the 1944-pattern infantry divisions, the men of this battalion were designated 'fusilier' and rode bicycles, but in the Panzer divisions they were heavily armed and used armoured cars and half-tracks.

It is interesting to note that, owing to the shortage of manpower, the establishment of all types of units suffered a continual reduction from mid-1943. From 1939 to 1943 the average division contained some sixteen thousand men. By 1945 this number had been reduced by about twenty-five per cent, but despite this the firepower of all types of units

German Panzer-grenadiers. These were the troops that formed the infantry element of the Panzer divisions.

had actually increased. This was achieved by taking full advantage of improvements in weapon technology – by the wide use of automatic weapons and the introduction of new types of armament such as the multi-barrelled rocket launcher, the '*Nebelwerfer*'.

The following weapon details cover some of the standard armaments in use by the German Army:

98 (7·9mm) rifle Effective range: 800 yards. 5-round magazine.

MP 40 machine pistol 100- and 200-metre (109- and 219-yard) fixed sights. 32-round magazine.

MG 34 standard light machine gun Effective range: 600–800 yards. When fixed to a tripod and used as a heavy machine gun, its effective range was 2,000–2,500 yards.

MG 42 standard light machine gun Similar in performance to the MG 34.

75mm field gun Maximum range: 12,570 yards. Muzzle velocity: 1,985 feet per second.

105mm medium gun Maximum range: 20,850 yards. Muzzle velocity: 2,740 feet per second.

150mm heavy gun Maximum range: 27,040 yards. Muzzle velocity: 2,838 feet per second.

37mm Pak. 38 anti-tank gun Muzzle velocity: 2,625 feet per second. Weight of shot: 1·5 pounds.

50mm Pak. 38 anti-tank gun Muzzle velocity: 2,740 feet per second. Weight of shot: 2·025 pounds.

75mm Pak. 40 anti-tank gun Muzzle velocity: 2,530 feet per second, using APCBC ammunition. Weight of shot: 15 pounds.

88mm Pak. 43/41 anti-tank gun Muzzle velocity: 3,705 feet per second, using AP40* ammunition; 3,280 feet per second using APCBC* ammunition. Weight of shot: AP40, 16 pounds; APCBC, 22·36 pounds.

Other anti-tank weapons in use with the German Army at the end of the war included a series of rocket-assisted, hollow-charge projectiles which were launched from simple tubes. The '*Panzerfaust*' and '*Panzerschreck*' were two such devices, both having relatively short ranges – 30 and 130 yards respectively. Both were, however, capable of penetrating over two hundred millimetres of homogeneous steel plate.

---

*AP = armour piercing; APCBC = armour-piercing capped ballistic cap.

The Italian Army

Of the six armies discussed in this section, the Italian was the least effective. It tended to be equipped with outdated and underpowered weapons, and, when committed to combat against other European armies, it proved itself unequal to the task.

Armoured divisions were relatively weak. They contained a mixture of light and medium tanks, none heavier than 11 tons, 165 in number grouped together in a tank regiment. Infantry support was provided by a single motorized regiment of *bersaglieri*, and the complement was made up with an anti-tank battalion, with eighteen guns; an artillery regiment; an engineer battalion, and supporting supply and medical units. The artillery regiment had six batteries of 75/27 guns; two of 105mm guns; two of 90/53 guns; two of 47mm anti-tank guns, and three of 20mm anti-tank/anti-aircraft weapons. Each battery had four pieces. In addition, the regiment had two self-propelled battalions with a total of twenty 75/18 guns mounted on M13/40 tank chassis, which were introduced into the division as a direct result of German influence.

Infantry divisions contained two infantry regiments and one of artillery, a mortar battalion, pioneer and signal com-

Italian soldiers, 1940–2. (*Left to right*) an infantryman; an artillery officer; an infantry corporal; an Alpine infantryman; and a *bersaglieri*.

panies, and supporting services. A Black Shirt legion, recruited from the Fascist militia and equivalent in strength to a battalion, was also included in the division's establishment. Each infantry regiment had a headquarters and three battalions; a battalion had four companies – one of heavy weapons and three of rifles. The rifle companies were formed from three rifle platoons, each of two sections, whereas the heavy-weapon company had one machine-gun platoon and two of 45mm mortars. The rifle sections each contained twenty men and included in their armament two light machine guns.

A comparison between the Italian and German establishments shows how comparatively weak the Italian units were. Although the full strength of an infantry division amounted to some twelve thousand five hundred men, the armoured divisions were only half that size.

The main Italian weapons are noted here, together with details of their performance:

6·5mm rifle, Model 91 (Mannlicher-Carcano) Sighted from 600 to 2,000 metres (656 to 2,187 yards). 6-round magazine.

6·5mm light machine gun, Model 30 (Breda) Sighted from 300 to 1,500 metres (328 to 1,640 yards); battle sights set at 300 metres (328 yards). 20-round magazine.

8mm medium machine gun, Model 35 (Fiat-Revelli) Sighted from 200 to 2,400 metres (219 to 2,625 yards). Fed by metal belts containing 50–250 rounds.

45mm mortar, Model 35 (Brixia) Maximum range: 586 yards. Rate of fire: 25–30 rounds per minute.

47/32 anti-tank gun, Model 37 Maximum range: 3,800 yards. Muzzle velocity: 2,067 feet per second. Weight of shot: 3·25 pounds. Rate of fire: 7–8 rounds per minute.

75/18 field gun Carried on self-propelled mounting. Maximum range: 10,280 yards.

75/27 field gun Maximum range: 11,000 yards.

90/53 dual-purpose anti-aircraft gun Mounted on the rear of a vehicle. Maximum horizontal range: 15,310 yards. Rate of fire: 20 rounds per minute.

105/32 field gun Maximum range: 17,500 yards.

Artillery types were designated by a figure indicating the calibre in millimetres, followed by the barrel length in calibres.

The Japanese Army

The Japanese Army was characterized by a fanaticism unknown in the Western world. It was a quality which sprang from the very roots of Japanese society – from the belief that Japan was of divine origin and that the Emperor was a god. Every Japanese was instilled with loyalty to his family, his community, the nation, and above all to the Emperor. The spirit of loyalty, self-sacrifice, and obedience produced soldiers who implicitly obeyed the orders of those set above them and who regarded death for their country, or Emperor, as a virtue. Conversely, to be taken prisoner was considered to be the ultimate degradation. This latter fact explains Japanese brutality to prisoners and, when coupled to the concept of patriotic death, accounts for the so-called 'Banzai' attacks and the consistent Japanese refusal to surrender, even in the most desperate of situations. Any wargame involving the Japanese Army must provide separate rules to cover this unique aspect of morale.

The Army had a divisional structure. All divisions were

Japanese soldiers, 1941–5. (*Left to right*) an officer in tropical dress; a private in tropical dress; two views of an infantryman in full equipment; and an officer in service dress.

roughly similar to infantry divisions in other armies, but the organization of each reflected its role and the terrain over which it was expected to fight. The actual composition of each division, and of its component parts, created an infinite number of variations on the accepted standard. The normal division contained an infantry group of three regiments; cavalry, artillery, engineer, and transport regiments; and signal, medical, ordnance, and veterinary sections. Tank units could form part of a division, and other units could also be attached. Likewise, divisional size could contract.

A standard infantry regiment consisted of three battalions, plus signals and anti-tank and infantry gun companies. The battalions all contained headquarters with train detachments, four companies, a machine-gun company, and an infantry gun platoon. A company comprised three platoons – each of three rifle sections (thirteen men with twelve rifles and a light machine gun) – and a grenade-discharger section armed with rifles and three 50mm small portable weapons. The machine-gun company had four platoons, one of which maintained the ammunition supply. The other three each consisted of four sections, with one heavy machine gun to every section. The infantry gun platoon had two sections, each with one gun.

The weapons listed here include the types most widely used by the Japanese:

Model 99 7·7mm rifle Sighted from 300 to 1,500 metres (328 to 1,640 yards). 5-round magazine.

Model 38 6·5mm rifle (Arisaka) Sighted from 100 to 2,400 metres (109 to 2,625 yards). 5-round magazine.

Model 96 6·5mm light machine gun Sighted from 200 to 1,500 metres (219 to 1,640 yards). 30-round magazine.

Model 92 7·7mm heavy machine gun Sighted from 300 to 2,700 metres (328 to 2,953 yards). Fed by 30-round ammunition strips.

Model 89 50mm grenade discharger Ranges between 120 and 670 metres (131 to 733 yards).

Model 41 75mm infantry gun Maximum range: 7,800 yards.

Model 38 75mm field gun Maximum range: 9,025 yards. Rate of fire: 8–10 rounds per minute.

Model 92 102mm gun Maximum range: 16,400 yards. Rate of fire: 6–8 rounds per minute.

Despite the tenacious defence of the Pacific Islands, it should be noted that Japanese tactics were based on the attack. Defence was considered a negative form of operation from which nothing was to be gained.

Naval and air power

Although wargames involving only land forces can be played, there comes a point at which, if one is striving for realism, the existence of naval and air forces cannot be ignored. In the Second World War, air power increasingly dominated land operations. The Allies' absolute control of the air over the

The effect of airpower on land warfare in the Second World War was nowhere more clearly illustrated than in the results obtained by fighter bombers against troop movements and transport columns.

Normandy battlefields in 1944 placed severe limitations on the German Army; it was forced to move by night and any vehicle which was seen by fighter bombers during the day survived only with luck. Control of the skies made possible the invasion of Normandy, but the success of the venture hung just as much on the ability of the Allied Fleet to dominate the English Channel and to protect the armies as they sailed towards their objective.

Air and sea wargames can be played in isolation or they can be integrated into an all-embracing scheme involving land forces. Strategic bombing and naval blockade form an essential part of any advanced wargame which takes into account the overall economic strength of a country.

There are direct parallels between wargames based on land and on sea warfare. Each ship has specific characteristics which determine movement and firepower, and it is a relatively simple task to discover that a particular warship had a speed of so many knots and that its principal and secondary armament consisted of certain specific guns. Like tanks, modern warships are armoured and the extent of this armour can be found in the standard reference works on the subject. It is the calculation of fire effect that presents certain problems in naval wargames and this is because of the completely unpredictable results that a shell can have. If shells were to strike key parts of a ship, the results could be decisive. A single shell penetrating to a ship's magazine would invariably result in a gigantic explosion which would literally tear the vessel apart. A direct hit on the steering mechanism could prevent a ship's course from being changed. If the fire-control equipment was destroyed, even the largest of ships would be effectively disarmed, ranging by manual controls being little better than useless for anything but short-range direct fire. Direct hits scored on guns would gradually diminish the fighting efficiency of a ship and hits of any nature would have a cumulative effect. However, since fire-control officers could not calculate exactly where the shells would fall, it is best to assess effect upon a random basis with only a slim chance of causing serious damage by a single shell.

Torpedoes were a much more effective weapon than shells since the latter seldom caused damage below the waterline,

Air and sea power: RAF Swordfish (torpedo bombers) launching an attack on a capital ship.

whereas the former always did, providing they hit. Torpedoes ran straight, at a set depth, to the limit of their range. A single hit was quite likely to sink a ship. They were carried on destroyers and some other surface craft, but their principal use was as the main armament of submarines.

Since submarine warfare was at first very much a battle of wits, its simulation must include this element. One way in which this can be achieved is to move the surface and under-water craft upon two separate maps or grids with an umpire adjudicating on contacts. Due provision must, however, be made for sounding equipment, such as ASDIC on the surface vessels; devices like radar and hydrophones should also be included.

Aircraft carriers formed the link between air and sea power. They were used extensively in the Pacific where it was proven that air power could be decisive in naval engagements. Set complements of aircraft were on board the different aircraft carriers and these facts are easily determined.

Aerial combat presents completely different problems from those encountered in land or sea wargames because it is, in effect, three dimensional. Aircraft at a higher level always enjoyed an initial advantage in the attack as they dived upon their enemy, but, once combat had been joined, success devolved upon the skill of the pilot and the excellence of his machine. By evaluating the performance of an aircraft (its rate of climb, speed, and turn capability) and by introducing a very short time-period for each move, such as a few seconds, the intricacies of a dog fight can be reproduced, but this is hardly worthwhile unless it is the object of the game. Aerial firepower was fairly effective if it hit the target, but this was not easy unless the fire was aimed from behind by an aircraft flying at approximately the same speed as the target. Fixed armament carried in the wings of aircraft was generally calibrated to converge at a point some two to three hundred yards ahead of the aircraft.

Heavy bombing aircraft mounted large numbers of machine guns and the Americans evolved a system of mutual support for their aircraft. The bombers would fly in large 'boxes' and the resultant fire from hundreds of machine guns made it difficult for an enemy fighter even to approach.

The accuracy of bombing depended upon locating the target. In thick cloud, results were erratic, but on a clear day they could be spectacular. British night bombing produced an élite 'Pathfinder' force which would locate the target and mark it with flares; other aircraft would then use these flares as an aiming point.

Both naval and air operations were influenced by the weather. High winds and low cloud could ground entire air forces for days; at sea, although large ships were more or less unaffected, small craft were in considerable danger and operations such as landings could not be conducted in adverse conditions.

BIBLIOGRAPHY

Most of the following books are generally available from publishers, bookshops, or through public libraries. However, a few may only be consulted in the libraries of military museums and similar institutions.

Wargaming

Advanced War Games by Donald Featherstone. Stanley Paul, London, 1969.

Battles with Model Soldiers by Donald Featherstone. David and Charles, Newton Abbot, 1970.

Charge! or How to Play Wargames by Peter Young and J.P. Lawford, Morgan-Grampian, West Wickham, 1967.

Little Wars by H.G. Wells. Reprinted by Arms and Armour Press, London, 1969.

Rules of Wargaming by A. Taylor. Shire Publications, Aylesbury, 1969.

The War Game by Charles Grant. A. & C. Black, London, 1971.

Wargame Campaigns by Donald Featherstone. Stanley Paul, London, 1970.

The Napoleonic Wars

The Anatomy of Glory: Napoleon and His Guard by Henri Lachouque, edited and translated by A.D.K. Brown. Lund Humphries, London, 1962.

The Background of Napoleonic Warfare: The Theory of Military Tactics in Eighteenth-Century France by Robert S. Quimby. Oxford University Press for Columbia, New York, 1952.

The Campaigns of Napoleon by David Chandler. Weidenfeld and Nicolson, London, 1967.

French Napoleonic Artillery by Michael Head. Almark, New Malden, 1970.

A Military History and Atlas of the Napoleonic Wars (2 volumes) edited by Vincent J. Esposito and John R. Elting. Faber, London, 1964.

Napoleon and Waterloo by A.F. Becke. Kegan Paul, London, 1939.

The Prussian Army, 1808–1815 by David Nash. Almark, London, 1972.

Regiments at Waterloo by René North. Almark, London, 1971.

Studies of the Napoleonic Wars by Charles Oman. Methuen, London, 1929.

American Civil War

American Civil War Cavalry by Michael Blake. Almark, London, 1973.

American Civil War Infantry by Michael Blake. Almark, London, 1970.

Arms and Equipment of the Civil War by Jack C. Coggins. Doubleday, New York, 1962.

Glory Road by Bruce Catton. Doubleday, New York, 1952.

Mr Lincoln's Army by Bruce Catton. Doubleday, New York, 1951.

A Stillness at Appomattox by Bruce Catton. Doubleday, New York, 1953.

Second World War

British and American Tanks of World War II by Peter Chamberlain and Chris Ellis. Arms and Armour Press, London, 1969.

German Army Handbook, 1939–1945 by W.J.K. Davies. Ian Allan, London, 1973.

German Tanks of World War II: Complete Illustrated History of German Armoured Fighting Vehicles 1926–45 by F.M. von Senger und Etterlin, translated by J. Lucas and edited by Peter Chamberlain. Arms and Armour Press, London, 1969.

The Guns, 1939–45 by Ian V. Hogg. History of the Second World War Series, Macdonald, London, 1970.

Handbook on the British Army compiled by the United States War Department, Washington, 1942.

Handbook on the German Military Forces compiled by the United States War Department, Washington, 1945. Republished by Founders Limited, Des Moines, Iowa, 1968.

Handbook on the Italian Military Forces compiled by the United States War Department, Washington, 1942.

Handbook on the Japanese Military Forces compiled by the United States War Department, Washington, 1944.

Die Panzergrenadier by F.M. von Senger und Etterlin. Lehmann, Munich, 1961.

INDEX

Figures in bold refer
to illustrations.

SOME OTHER TITLES IN THIS SERIES

Arts
Antique Furniture/Architecture/Art Nouveau for Collectors/Clocks and Watches/Glass for Collectors/Jewellery/Musical Instruments/ Porcelain/Pottery/Silver for Collectors/Victoriana

Domestic Animals and Pets
Budgerigars/Cats/Dog Care/Dogs/Horses and Ponies/Pet Birds/Pets for Children/Tropical Freshwater Aquaria/Tropical Marine Aquaria

Domestic Science
Flower Arranging

Gardening
Chrysanthemums/Garden Flowers/Garden Shrubs/House Plants/ Plants for Small Gardens/Roses

General Information
Aircraft/Arms and Armour/Coins and Medals/Espionage/Flags/ Fortune Telling/Freshwater Fishing/Guns/Military Uniforms/Motor Boats and Boating/National Costumes of the world/Orders and Decorations/Rockets and Missiles/Sailing/Sailing Ships and Sailing Craft/Sea Fishing/Trains/Veteran and Vintage Cars/Warships

History and Mythology
Age of Shakespeare/Archaeology/Discovery of: Africa/The American West/Australia/Japan/North America/South America/Great Land Battles/Great Naval Battles/Myths and Legends of: Africa/Ancient Egypt/Ancient Greece/Ancient Rome/India/The South Seas/ Witchcraft and Black Magic

Natural History
The Animal Kingdom/Animals of Australia and New Zealand/ Animals of Southern Asia/Bird Behaviour/Birds of Prey/Butterflies/ Evolution of Life/Fishes of the world/Fossil Man/A Guide to the Seashore/Life in the Sea/Mammals of the world/Monkeys and Apes/Natural History Collecting/The Plant Kingdom/Prehistoric Animals/Seabirds/Seashells/Snakes of the world/Trees of the world/Tropical Birds/Wild Cats

Popular Science
Astronomy/Atomic Energy/Chemistry/Computers at Work/The Earth/Electricity/Electronics/Exploring the Planets/Heredity/ The Human Body/Mathematics/Microscopes and Microscopic Life/ Physics/Psychology/Undersea Exploration/The Weather Guide